GETTING JUSTICE

GETTING JUSTICE

The Rights of People

STEPHEN GILLERS

BASIC BOOKS, INC., PUBLISHERS

NEW YORK   LONDON

11-8-72

FOREWORD

by Ramsey Clark

A people who do not know their rights have little advantage over those who have none. Rights are not self-enforcing. They are rarely significantly stronger or weaker than the commitment of the people in heart and mind to their fulfillment. A society which cares so little about its rights that the individuals who comprise it do not come to know their own can never instill such a fierce devotion to the rule of law in the enforcers that they will insist on the protection of the poor, the powerless, the ignorant, the sick, and the deprived.

If we are to live with dignity and peace in the complexities of a mass, urban, technologically advanced society, the law must become a sensitive and effective instrument for social change. This will not happen unless the citizenry is thoroughly involved. To be a just society we must create a panoply of rights adequate to human needs and strive constantly to perfect, simplify, and fulfill those rights.

The quest begins with an understanding of present rights. What are they? Are they sufficient to human dignity? Are they in fact fulfilled for all? In what ways shall they be changed or enlarged that they may meet the needs of the people? Now, finally, do we really implement adequate rights equally for all? These issues must be the great concern of a nation.

Only an informed concern can lead to constructive action.

This important book is one of a number that understands the absolute necessity for involving the people in the perfection and fulfillment of rights.

The central question of our time is human dignity. Can it be developed and preserved in mass society? The ultimate attack on human dignity arises in the contest between the individual and the state when the power of the people through government is used unfairly to attack those it fears or hates. The development of rules of criminal procedure which can protect human dignity amidst the complexities of advanced technology and population explosion will require the involvement, understanding, and contribution of those who most passionately seek social change. Foremost among these are the young, the minorities, and the poor. It is, after all, they who experience the most intense conflict between man and his state, and it is their rights and freedom that the forces of history place in greatest jeopardy. It is their rights and freedom that the just society must protect most generously and ardently. The public, generous in purpose, when uninformed of the truth of the confrontation between the individual and his government, will never overcome emotion and demagoguery. Those who seek change will be resisted with force, justice will be forgotten and the rule of law will fail.

The case of *Miranda* v. *Arizona* offers an interesting illustration. Probably no decision by the United States Supreme Court during the turbulent 1960s caused greater misunderstanding and apprehension. But consider—the court ruled only that the police should advise a person suspected of crime of his rights. If we believe in rights, can we really want the police to do otherwise? The rights of which a suspect must be advised under *Miranda* are the rights to counsel, the right to free legal assistance if he cannot afford counsel, the right to remain silent, and the right of the state to use admissions or confessions in a court of law. Need the police advise the rich of such rights? Of course not. The police would not transgress the rights of the rich because they know that lawyers will soon appear and their work will be undone to the peril of the case and perhaps their own careers. Need the police advise the mobster or the hardened criminal of such rights? Of course not—he knows them. So, too, the educated man and the plain person with common sense know, however frightened they may be at the moment, that they can remain silent. Who then is left but the poor, the ignorant, the sick, and the weak. Have we so little sense of justice that we would take advantage of these? The price, if we do, is enormous. People will not respect the rule of law because it acts immorally.

Ironically, effective law enforcement suffers greatly from such abuses because experience clearly shows that scientific investigation will not use interrogation as a significant instrument for finding truth. It is slow, unreliable, and wasteful. The FBI on its own initiative, in the interest of effective investigation, began giving the essentials of the *Miranda* warning in 1948, eighteen years before the Supreme Court pronounced its rule. No one has criticized the FBI for being soft on crime because of this; nor has its conviction rate suffered.

As a further irony, there has been no demonstration of any impairment to prosecution as a result of *Miranda*. Miranda himself was subsequently convicted on the same indictment without the use in evidence of the confession taken in violation of his rights. So were all of the other defendants whose cases were reversed that same day. Of greatest concern, however, and fundamentally questioning our commitment to the rule of law, is the fact that despite all the controversy about the *Miranda* decision, it is generally ignored in police conduct. Had the public adequate understanding of the real meaning of the Fifth Amendment, the nature of crime, and the neglect of law enforcement, its outrage would not have been that the Supreme Court finally announced the fundamental justice of *Miranda* but that we as a nation had not insisted on it all along.

Wiretapping and electronic surveillance offer another illustration of the need of the people for sophisticated understanding of the elements of freedom and human dignity. American citizens enjoyed no protection from what Justice Holmes called "a dirty business"—in the 1928 *Olmstead* decision—until the administrative restrictions on Federal electronics surveillance were imposed by President Johnson in 1965. Subsequent Supreme Court decisions now afford some constitutional protection. But the battle to preserve privacy from the nearly total invasion technology makes possible is being lost and will continue to be until the people insist upon the integrity of the rights of every individual—rights that are adequate to his dignity.

Steve Gillers is one of that new breed of young American lawyers deeply concerned about justice, freedom, and dignity. He has brought a bold and imaginative mind to the task of "Getting Justice" in America. For your own sake and the future of freedom you should read this book, read it carefully and go on from here to others so that you may help create in the people an understanding of the elements of justice and a passion for securing it for all. What we must understand if this is to be is that mere words on paper have substance only through the actions of the people. The truth of the Bill of Rights will abide. The question is, will we?

ACKNOWLEDGMENTS

This modest book is meant to give nonlawyers (and lawyers un-familiar with the area) an introduction to the *what* and *why* of the criminal process. These are the things I wanted to know about before law school, but about which I could find no basic book to tell me. I have tried, therefore, consistent with accuracy, to be simple and straightforward.

But even simple books, I've learned, are the products of many minds and much assistance. Hon. Gus J. Solomon, Chief Judge of the Federal District Court in Portland, Oregon, taught me things in my year's work with him that could easily fill another volume. For this reason, and many others, I fondly dedicate this book to him.

I am also grateful to Arthur Liman and Hon. Irving Younger, both of whom read (in record time) an earlier manuscript and made valuable suggestions. I should add that there is no better place to test one's possible defense-bias than with two former federal prosecutors.

I am grateful also to Bill Gum at Basic Books both for his interest, and for his important suggestions, at a critical point, on overall structure. I am particularly thankful because Bill's advice always came over a great lunch.

Finally, I thank Ina Gillers, my wife, for her ongoing help and criticism. She was the ideal layman and stopped me whenever my writing drifted into legalese.

Of course, all shortcomings in the following pages remain mine.

STEPHEN GILLERS

New York, N.Y.
February 25, 1971

CONTENTS

GETTING JUSTICE

I

PERSPECTIVE

AND

INTRODUCTION

Society has the power to define certain acts as criminal and to provide sanctions against the actor. This power is probably necessary for the survival of any nation. Nevertheless, there are limits to the power which are as important as the power itself because they determine the nature of our society and the quality of life within it. This book is about the limits. It is about the relationship between the individual and the state in the enforcement of criminal law.

There are two good, practical reasons to write this book. The most important is to make people aware of their rights. The man-on-the-street may be the first to say, "I've got my rights," but the last to know what they are. The police and the courts must follow rules. It is important to the overall efficient administration of justice that people have some knowledge of the rules.

Many people think a policeman can do almost anything he pleases. Many policemen think this too, but there are rules, developed and refined across centuries, that carefully define the policeman's power to enforce the law.

I once saw a middle-aged woman walking with two teenage girls through Washington Square Park in New York City's Greenwich Village. An antiwar demonstration was scheduled later that day and several police cars and paddy wagons lined the street just ahead of the woman and the two girls. The woman mechanically started to cross the street. The two girls refused to follow.

"Walk on the other side," the woman called to the girls.

"Why? We're not doing anything wrong," one responded. The woman crossed the street and the two girls continued on past the police cars. The woman's apprehensive reaction to state authority should be the exception in a constitutional democracy. However, it is probably the rule in the United States.

Many argue that the police should not be handcuffed when they fight crime. Crime is not good for society, why should society be good to crime? Politicians often revert to this argument, with its surface logic, at election time. Crime is something everyone is against, so it's all right to be as merciless toward it as we can.

This argument has emotional appeal for many. Unfortunately, the opposing argument is subtle and difficult to appreciate. It will be developed more fully later in this chapter. Essentially it is that the rules which the "unhandcuffers" argue protect criminals protect us all. When we ignore the rules because we think that will make catching criminals more efficient, we increase the potential for abuse of power.[1] We must carefully weigh what we're giving up against what we're getting because as the rules drop away, we come closer to a police state. In a police state, the police are not answerable to the people, but only to themselves.

This prospect seems comparatively unreal to the unhand-

---

[1] In reading a prior draft of this Chapter, a colleague felt it suggested the view that adherence to constitutional guarantees would necessarily be at the expense of efficient law enforcement. I do not believe this, and I have tried to correct that impression. On the other hand, it may happen that observance of a defendant's constitutional rights will require the court to acquit someone who "did it." Perhaps this is "inefficient" law enforcement if the only goal is conviction. But, for reasons discussed later, I think it is preferable to accept this type of "inefficiency" in return for other societal benefits.

cuffers, who each day read of very real increases in criminal activity. They argue that theoretical hodgepodge about police states should not make us unduly solicitous of the rights of criminals. It should be emphasized that the rules we shall discuss are not meant to protect criminals. They are meant to protect people from an arbitrary abuse of power. No person in our society is a criminal until he is found, beyond a reasonable doubt, to be guilty of a crime in a court of law, or until his guilty plea is accepted by a judge. If all policemen had a sixth sense that enabled them to pick out the criminals among us *and only the criminals,* then we might have developed a different system of criminal justice. But policemen have no such powers. Consequently, when a judge demands that the police respect a suspect's constitutional rights, this demand will ultimately affect the millions of police-citizen contacts that occur each year, but which result in no official action.

Americans have always been suspicious of power. We divide power not only among three branches of government on the federal level, but also between the federal and state levels. Each state further divides its power among three governmental branches. I believe the underlying assumption is that great concentrations of power should be tolerated as infrequently as possible; and when it is necessary in order to get things done for a man or group of men to have power over the lives of others, the exercise of this power should be subject to control and review.

I have hinted at the second reason for this book. Outcries against recent United States Supreme Court decisions are frequently voiced. Many responsible people charge the Court with "coddling criminals." But critics cannot constructively discuss the opinions of the Court unless they read and understand them within a larger context. To hear that the Court has ordered the release of a convicted criminal may be alarming. However, one cannot adequately criticize, or appreciate, the Court's rulings until he understands why this is done, in view of the overall structure of our criminal procedure as it has developed over the centuries and is still developing today.

We read in the newspaper that a court has ordered a new trial for a convicted burglar (or rapist, since that is the constant example of the unhandcuffers). We read that at the defendant's first trial the evidence against him was overwhelming. We're amazed, and we wonder why this fellow was given a new trial, with the possibility of acquittal, when his guilt is evident. We read on and we learn that the court ordered the new trial because the signed confession introduced in evidence against the alleged burglar (or rapist) at the first trial was the product of a day and a half of police interrogation, when the accused was not permitted to see or speak to a lawyer or a member of his family, or receive adequate food, medication, or sleep. The court held that the confession was not voluntary and, therefore, should not have been allowed in evidence against the accused. At the next trial, it must be excluded from evidence, even if the exclusion results in the likelihood of acquittal.

All right, perhaps a confession that results from coercive conditions should be excluded because it is unreliable. The suspect may have confessed falsely in order to satisfy his hunger, fatigue, or medical needs. Certainly a confession that follows a beating is untrustworthy. Perhaps strong psychological coercion is also likely to produce a false confession.

But what about a confession given after only an hour of interrogation and excluded merely because the police failed to tell the suspect that he had a right to an attorney, or that if he could not afford an attorney he would be assigned one free, or that he had a right to remain silent, or that anything he said may be held against him? In such a case, is there any serious contention that the confession is unreliable? The answer, generally, is no—although research by social psychologists and lawyers has shown that even under noncoercive circumstances, some people will confess *in detail* to acts they have never done.[2]

If a noncoerced confession is apparently reliable (as when there is corroborative evidence), why exclude it simply because the police failed to warn the suspect of his rights before the questioning? The answer is only superficially related to "the law," or even "justice." It has something to do with the way we choose to treat the individual in his relationship with the state. A man should not have to testify against himself, incriminate, or accuse himself, and the state should not be permitted to make him do so. If he wants to confess, or plead guilty to a crime, he may, but only if his action is voluntary. Voluntariness means choice and choice means a knowledge of the alternatives. If a person does not know that he has a right to an attorney—even if he cannot afford one—or that he does not have to answer questions, his "decision" to confess is not voluntary. He has incriminated himself without a full knowledge of the alternatives, and ignorance of these alternatives makes his confession inadmissible. This result is more compelling when we realize that those who are unaware of the alternatives are usually poor and uneducated.

But what do we care if a confession is technically involuntary? That is just a label we use in order to reach a result we have decided is proper. But is it proper? The state, after all, did not do anything really shocking when it failed to inform the suspect of his right to an attorney. And the suspect has confessed to a burglary or a rape. Assuming the confession is reliable, that it is not the product of psychological or physical force, why let this fellow off merely because we forgot to warn him of a constitutional right? Isn't our reaction extreme in light of the comparatively slight technical error of the police? Wouldn't a reprimand to the interrogating officer suffice?

[2] See, for example, Driver, "Confessions and the Social Psychology of Coercion," 82 *Harvard Law Review* 42 (1968); Raab, *Justice in the Back Room* (1967).

These questions assume that the exclusion of a confession is the reward society pays the suspect because it erred in his case. In part, it is true that the exclusion is meant to honor the suspect's constitutional right against self-incrimination. But, as the next few paragraphs try to explain, we also exclude the confession because of the long-term advantages to society generally. In addition, reprimands and other remedies short of exclusion have been ineffective in controlling police conduct. Finally, we must always remember that transgressions against "bad guys" represent only the top of the iceberg. By responding to these transgressions, the courts also protect the numerous innocent persons who may temporarily be suspected of criminal activity, but whose cases never reach the judicial stage.

We have used the example of a coerced confession in discussing the reasons a court might exclude otherwise reliable evidence. We could have used other examples, such as evidence seized after an unlawful search. There is an underlying rationale: the respect we feel the state must have for the individual and his privacy, a respect which must keep the state from turning the individual against himself. A man has a right to draw lines around his mind, his home, his relationship with his wife, etc., and we want to be very careful before we allow the state to trespass across those lines. Under certain conditions we will allow it, but only because we believe the reasons for allowing it are more compelling than the opposing reasons.

So, for example, we will permit the authorities to search a man's home or person if there is probable cause to believe they will find something. Suspicion alone is not enough to justify this degree of intrusion. But neither do we require certainty. We balance the nature of the invasion of privacy against the likelihood of success. When the invasion of privacy is less—a frisk of outer clothing for weapons, for example—we permit the intrusion on grounds less than probable cause. The balance changes. In our confession example, the court has decided that conviction of the guilty is a less important value than a person's right to know his constitutional options before he is interrogated. Rights do not belong only to those fortunate enough to be aware of them.

The subtlety of this reasoning sometimes prevents us from understanding a court's action. How much, we ask, will the dignity of man in the United States suffer if a single trespass against the privacy of a particular criminal is ignored and he is kept in jail? In any one situation it is true that the dignity of man will not erode if we ignore the state invasion that produced, for example, the involuntary confession, and keep the criminal in jail. The danger is the erosion that will occur when the state is allowed to trespass across private lines without check. For although it may never happen to us, good, law-abiding citizens, we come to realize as these trespasses accumulate, that we live in a society where this sort of thing happens, where government can ignore privacy with impunity and without consequence. And this knowledge will inevitably affect concepts of privacy and of the dignity of the individual within the greater, noncriminal world. No man can feel safe in his private life or respect the private lives of others when he knows that his government is free to invade the private lives and minds of those it suspects of criminal activity. The power of government to invade privacy in the criminal area will inevitably have an effect on the nature of privacy and the quality of life in every area.[3]

This is not a new problem, but one as old as civilization. A balance must be reached between the needs of the people to protect themselves from antisocial conduct and the needs of each person to protect himself from a group action that invades his privacy and affronts his dignity. Neither the people nor any single person is entitled to have his demands prevail at any cost. The question is where along the continuum do we stop. It is not an easy decision to make because of the subtle, prac-

[3] See, Alan F. Westin, *Privacy and Freedom* (New York: Atheneum, 1967).

tically undefinable values at stake and because the promise of efficient law enforcement for the compromise of constitutional rights is baseless. And the decision is never finally made; each day our values change. This book will try to identify where along the continuum we have landed in the past so that we may make decisions more intelligently in the future.

This book is not intended to be a substitute for a lawyer, in much the same way that a first-aid book is not intended to substitute for a doctor. All one can do is discuss past cases which have indicated future rules. The reader can learn generally what his rights are and how the rules of criminal procedure operate. However, no one should use this book as a do-it-yourself kit. Law is a changing thing. Lawyers are trained to apply past cases to present conflicts, whereas laymen are not. Although there is some danger that a few will use this book for the wrong reasons, the dangers that flow from a public ignorant of its rights are greater.

Chapters 2 through 9 examine the criminal process in three different ways. Chapters 2 and 3 are concerned with the over-all political, historical and legal structure within which the criminal process operates. Chapters 4 through 8 analyze the various rules of constitutional criminal procedure. Finally, Chapter 9 discusses two of the ways in which the Constitution's demands are informally compromised.

2

THE STRUCTURE
OF THE
CRIMINAL PROCESS

This chapter will consider the legal and political structure within which the criminal process operates. It will (1) enumerate the rules of criminal procedure contained in the Constitution and the Bill of Rights, (2) discuss the nature and function of the Supreme Court, and (3) briefly consider how the rules and the Court actually operate in the day-to-day criminal system. This chapter is intended to provide a framework for the more detailed discussions that follow it.

The Bill of Rights

Although the fifty states and the federal government each have different rules of criminal procedure, it is not necessary, for the purposes of this book, to study the particular rules in each of fifty-one jurisdictions. The United States Constitution demands that every jurisdiction governed by it comply with certain constitutional requirements, and it is these requirements that are a starting point for any inquiry into the criminal process.

The Constitution, written in 1787 and ratified two years later, placed few restrictions on the power of the federal government in its relations with the people. There was concern that this document, loaded with checks and balances, contained no check to prevent the arbitrary exercise of federal power against the individual. In reaction to this concern, James Madison made the following speech in Congress on June 8, 1789.

It cannot be a secret to the gentlemen in this House, that notwithstanding the ratification of this system of Government by eleven of the thirteen United States, in some cases unanimously, in others by large majorities; yet still there is a great number of our constituents who are dissatisfied with it; among whom are many respectable for their talents and patriotism, and respectable for the jealousy they have for their liberty, which, though mistaken in its object, is laudable in its motive. There is a great body of the people falling under this description, who at present feel much inclined to join their support to the cause of Federalism, if they were satisfied on this one point. We ought not to disregard their inclination, but, on principles of amity and moderation, conform to their wishes, and expressly declare the great rights of mankind secured under this constitution. The acquiescence which our fellow-citizens show under the Government, calls upon us for a like return of moderation. . . .

It may be that all paper barriers against the power of the community are too weak to be worthy of attention. . . . If they are incorporated into the constitution, independent tribunals of justice will consider themselves in a peculiar manner the guardians of those rights; they will be an impenetrable bulwark against every assumption of power in the legislative or executive; they will be naturally led to resist every encroachment upon rights expressly stipulated for in the constitution by the declaration of rights. . . .

I wish also, in revising the constitution . . . to . . . add . . . that no State shall violate the equal right of conscience, freedom of the press, or trial by jury in criminal cases; because it is proper that every Government should be disarmed of power which trench upon those particular rights. I know, in some of the State constitutions, the power of the Government is controlled by such a declaration; but others are not. I cannot see any reason against obtaining even a double security on these points. . . . It must be admitted . . . that the State Governments are as liable to attack these invaluable privileges as the General Government is, and therefore ought to be as cautiously guarded against.

Madison envisioned that the Bill of Rights would provide a "double security"—against both federal and state power. Nevertheless, the first eight amendments only limited federal power. The people would have to rely on their respective state constitutions for protection against the arbitrary use of state or local power. Not until 1868, when the Fourteenth Amendment was passed, did there appear the necessary legal machinery to apply many of the same restrictions and limitations to the states that amendments one through eight applied to the federal government nearly a century earlier. As we shall see, the Supreme Court has used this legal machinery extensively. Today, the states are bound by almost all of the criminal process requirements contained in the first eight amendments.

The constitutional rules of criminal procedure are contained in two sections of the original Constitution and five of the amendments (see Appendix B). Each rule is restated here in simple language, with its source in parentheses:

1. The federal government may not suspend the writ of habeas corpus for persons whose freedom is limited as a result of federal power. There is one exception. The writ of habeas corpus may be suspended if (1) there is either rebellion or invasion and (2) during such rebellion or invasion the public safety requires a suspension of the writ (Art. I, Sec. 9).

2. Except for impeachment, all federal crimes will be tried by a jury (Art. III, Sec. 1).

3. All federal trials will be held in the state where the crime was committed (Art. III, Sec. 1).

4. People have a right to not have their persons, houses, papers, and effects unreasonably searched or seized by the federal government (4th Am.).

5. Search warrants and arrest warrants can be issued to federal officers only on probable cause. The officer seeking the

warrant must swear or affirm that the information he is giving in order to receive the warrant is true (4th Am.).

6. A search warrant or arrest warrant issued to a federal officer must specifically describe the place to be searched or the persons or things to be seized (4th Am.).

7. In order to charge a person with a serious federal crime, there must be a Grand Jury indictment. However, this rule does not apply to crimes committed in the land or naval forces or in the militia when the alleged criminal is in actual service and it is a time of war or of public danger (5th Am.).

8. No person charged with committing a federal crime may be placed in jeopardy more than once for the same offense (5th Am.).

9. No person may be forced by the federal government to be a witness against himself or incriminate himself (5th Am.).

10. The federal government may not deprive any person of his life, liberty, or property, except with due process of law (5th Am.).

11. In criminal prosecutions in federal courts, the defendant has a right to a speedy trial (6th Am.).

12. A person charged with a federal crime has the right to a public trial (6th Am.).

13. A person charged with a federal crime has the right to be tried by an impartial jury (6th Am.).

14. Federal trials must take place in the state and district where the crime occurred (6th Am.).

15. A person charged with a federal crime is entitled to know the nature and cause of the charges against him and to be confronted with the witnesses against him (6th Am.).

16. A person charged with a federal crime has a right to compel witnesses in his favor to testify at his trial (6th Am.).

17. A person charged with a federal crime has the right to have the assistance of counsel for his defense (6th Am.).

18. The federal government may not impose excessive bail (8th Am.).

19. The federal government may not impose an excessive fine (8th Am.).

20. The federal government may not inflict cruel and unusual punishments (8th Am.).

21. No state may deprive any person of his life, liberty, or property, except with due process of law (14th Am.).

22. No state may deny anyone in its jurisdiction the equal protection of its laws (14th Am.).

Rules 1, 2, and 3 are in the original Constitution; they do not apply to the states. Rules 4 through 20 are contained in the Bill of Rights and, as originally written, restricted only the federal government. It is rule 21 that enables the Supreme Court to apply to the states many of the limitations on criminal law enforcement that the first eight amendments apply to the federal government. Section One of the Fourteenth Amendment (rule 21) says, in part, that no state may "deprive any person of life, liberty, or property without due process of law." Phrased positively, this clause permits denial of life, liberty, or property so long as it is accomplished with "due process of law."

Due process of law is not susceptible to easy definition. Indeed, as we shall see in the next chapter, its definition changes from time to time. Because the meaning of "due process" is vague and its location is critical, the Supreme Court has the legal power to control the criminal process in all fifty states. If the Court says due process of law includes the right to a jury trial in criminal cases, then no state may deprive any person of his life, liberty, or property in a criminal proceeding without a jury trial. If the Court says due process of law means the right to be assisted by counsel, appointed or retained, then all fifty states must abide by this rule before they can send a man to jail. Legally, the Court is free to fill in the blank (due process) with any rules a majority of Justices agrees belong there. Politically, as we shall discuss, this is not entirely so.

Unlike the Due Process Clause, the Equal Protection Clause

(rule 22) does not require the states to follow one particular rule or another, that is, it does not say certain rules are constitutionally required. Rather, it deals with how a state must apply the rules it does have—equally. This does not mean a state may never treat persons differently, but that persons in the same situation must be treated the same. An example will make this clear.

In *Griffin* v. *Illinois,* 351 U.S. 12 (1956),[1] two poor defendants were convicted of armed robbery in an Illinois court. They wanted to appeal their convictions to a State appellate court but were unable to prepare the necessary documents without a stenographic transcript of the trial proceedings. A transcript is expensive and the defendants asked the State to pay for it. The State refused with the explanation that it only paid for transcripts when the death sentence was involved. The defendants petitioned the United States Supreme Court for review. They argued that the Illinois rule deprived them of equal protection. The Supreme Court, agreeing, said:

Surely no one would contend that either a State or Federal Government could constitutionally provide that defendants unable to pay court costs in advance should be denied the right to plead not guilty or to defend themselves in court. Such a law would make the constitutional promise of a fair trial a worthless thing. . . . In criminal trials a State can no more discriminate on account of poverty than on account of religion, race, or color.

There is no meaningful distinction between a rule which would deny the poor the right to defend themselves in a trial court and one which effectively denies the poor an adequate appellate review accorded to all who have money enough to pay the costs in advance. It is true that a State is not required by the Federal Constitution to provide appellate courts or a right to appellate review at all. . . . But that is not to say that a State that does grant appellate review

---

[1] All Supreme Court opinions are printed in the *United States Reports,* among other places. The citation to *Griffin* v. *Illinois* means the opinion in that case can be found in volume 351 of the *United States Reports,* on page 12. The date in parenthesis is the year the case was decided. Parallel rules apply to citations from lower courts.

can do so in a way that discriminates against some convicted defendants on account of their poverty.

There can be no equal justice where the kind of trial a man gets depends on the amount of money he has. Destitute defendants must be afforded as adequate appellate review as defendants who have money enough to buy transcripts.

A rich man and a poor man convicted of crimes stand in the same position. The only difference between them is financial; but a state cannot allow this difference to result in the rich man having access to an appellate process and not the poor man. It must pay the poor man's way to make certain that persons in equal positions receive the equal protection of the law.

A state may treat persons differently when they occupy different positions, if there is a reasonable relationship between the difference in positions and the difference in treatment. For example, one indigent man may be accused of armed robbery, and another of embezzlement. They stand charged with different crimes. But that difference will not justify giving the first man a free attorney while denying the same right to the second man. On the other hand, if the armed robber is penniless and the embezzler is a millionaire, the state may supply the first with legal help and require the second to pay for his own. The difference in treatment is rationally related to the difference in position.

The Supreme Court has the same latitude when it deals with the Equal Protection Clause as it has when it defines due process. There are two basic questions to answer when a law is challenged on equal protection grounds. Is the state treating two people unequally? If so, is there a difference in the positions of the two people which reasonably justifies unequal treatment? Each of these questions gives the Court much room in which to move.

Although the Fourteenth Amendment contains both a Due Process and an Equal Protection Clause, the Fifth Amendment contains only the former. But this does not mean the United States may treat persons in equal circumstances unequally. In *Bolling* v. *Sharpe,* 347 U.S. 497 (1954), the Supreme Court held that the Due Process Clause of the Fifth Amendment implicitly contains an equal protection requirement.

The Supreme Court

It quickly becomes obvious that the Supreme Court is at the center of the development of the constitutional rules which govern the criminal process. Most of the rules the Court must define are vague and susceptible to several interpretations. For this reason, it is important to review briefly the position and role of the Supreme Court in the U.S. governmental structure.

The Court's power is divided among nine men, but only a majority of five is needed to make an interpretation of the Constitution the supreme law of the land. The character of the men who sit on the Court and the limits of the political process generally protect against arbitrary and capricious use of the Court's power. Though reasonable men may disagree on the outcome in any one case, most would concede that the Court has been conscientious in its attempt to define the limits of the criminal process. Nevertheless, the constitutionality of a particular state action depends on what the members of the Court consider "due process of law" to mean when the question arises.

To recognize the flexibility of the process is not to demean it. It is largely the same overall flexibility that has permitted the Constitution as a whole, with comparatively few changes, to govern the United States of 1789 and the United States of the 1970s—two very different countries.

Flexibility is necessary, but it alone does not guarantee success. Equally important is the self-restraint of those who exercise the power that flexibility creates. Ultimately, the problem is political because, in the end, law and politics are concerned with the same thing: the way of life of a people. While it is true that the value to society of general obedience to the law is greater than the inconvenience a particular law might cause, this truth is only general. The likelihood of obedience to any particular law will decrease as the law becomes repugnant to the values and attitudes of those who must obey it. One example, devoid of ideological overtones, is the Prohibition Amendment.

If, on the other hand, the Court concludes that the law requires a specific result, how long should it permit political considerations to influence the amount of time it waits before announcing its conclusion? The South still may not be politically receptive to the 1954 school desegregation cases, and it may be years before the country is willing to accept the school prayer cases; yet, in these examples, the Court would have betrayed its function in our system of government had it allowed popular wishes to influence its timing in securing the rights of minorities.

But timing and sensitivity to the nation's mood are still important. If judicial power is abused, or if groups within the nation feel that it is, recourse to the political process is inevitable. For example, Congress may narrow the jurisdiction of the federal courts, or the people may amend the Constitution to change one of the Court's interpretations. Such recourse, however, has not often been necessary.

It is essentially antidemocratic to allow nine men to decide what rules the remainder of the population will have to obey. Other things being equal, it would seem fairer for Congress or state legislatures to hold this power. A legislative body is more representative of the people than is the Supreme Court, whose appointed members serve for life. But the power does lie with the Court, not with Congress; one of the reasons this is preferable is that the Court is better able to protect the rights of minorities in face of majority antagonism. Momentary but intense emotional feeling, coupled with a legislative majority, has too often resulted in emasculation of the rights of a minority that happens to be on the "out." The Court, however, is expected to remain cool and act as a restraint on the corner-cutting that often accompanies self-righteousness.

The Court must be cautious before it speaks because its tool is constitutional interpretation. Once the Court has defined due process to mean one thing or another, Congress and the states cannot change this meaning through legislation. The time-consuming and undesirable constitutional amendment process is the sole remedy (short of a judicial about-face). Obviously, then, the Court has a difficult task: it must protect the rights of sometimes-detested minorities without frustrating the legitimate requirements and rights of the majority, and it must manage this balance with the awareness that its decisions are rarely subject to popular control within the current political structure.

The Court has chosen to define due process mainly in terms of the particular safeguards of the Bill of Rights (rules 4 to 20).[2] These safeguards are not the whimsical creations of nine men who happen, at any one time, to occupy the Court's nine seats. Rather, they have developed across centuries of Anglo-American history and jurisprudence, and they were placed in the Bill of Rights because of their overwhelming importance to the founders of the United States. The Court has not been arbitrary, careless, or ahistorical in determining what rules will limit the states in the enforcement of the criminal law.

By looking to the Bill of Rights for the meaning of due process, the Court has not forsaken flexibility. The limitations in the Bill of Rights are fairly vague. For example, who can define, without a look at the cases (or even with one), the meaning of "unreasonable" in the Fourth Amendment (rule

[2] As Chapter 3 indicates, this approach to the definitional problem is recent and has its opponents.

4)? The Court still retains the freedom it needs to define and redefine, as the nature of our society changes, the outer limits of the criminal process.

The Court, as we shall show, has not relied exclusively on the first eight amendments for the meaning of due process. Due process also requires that the states and the federal government act with fundamental fairness in the administration of criminal justice. If a state or the United States adopts a procedure that is fundamentally unfair, though not specifically proscribed by the first eight amendments, the procedure will be judged a denial of due process of law and unconstitutional. What is "fundamental fairness?"

The Criminal Process in Operation

In an attempt to understand the structure of the criminal process, we have briefly reviewed the rules in the Bill of Rights and the Fourteenth Amendment[3] and we have discussed the nature of the Supreme Court, the institution that has the ultimate responsibility to define and apply those rules. The remainder of this Chapter will outline the structure within which the rules and the institution operate.[4]

In response to a citizen's complaint, a suspect may be arrested on a warrant or sent a summons to appear in court at some future time. The complaint may also come from the policeman who observes a crime. Often the arrest will take place on the scene, and the complaint will follow. If arrested, the suspect may be released on bail at any time. In addition, the state may be required at a preliminary hearing to show

---

[3] These rules are extensively discussed in Chapters 3 through 8.
[4] A Flow Chart of the criminal process is printed in Appendix C.

probable cause for believing that the suspect committed a crime. If probable cause is shown, a formal charge—either a grand jury indictment, if that is required, or a prosecutor's information—may be filed. The suspect will appear in court for a formal arraignment, at which he will be asked to plead, probably for the first time. If he pleads guilty, he will be sentenced soon after. If he pleads not guilty, he will be tried and, if found guilty, the court will sentence him. The defendent may appeal from conviction on a not guilty plea, and in some cases on a guilty plea. Sentencing may include confinement or probation or a combination of both. Probation is "supervised freedom" ordered by the court. Parole is supervised freedom ordered by a parole board, which may decide that an incarcerated prisoner can be released before his time expires. Finally, while in jail, on probation, or on parole, the defendant may seek release through habeas corpus.

The above description is general, and the process may vary from state to state. The process is considerably simpler for misdemeanors than for felonies, and simpler still for petty offenses than for misdemeanors. The difference between the three types of crime is one of degree of seriousness. At any stage of the process, the suspect may be "discharged" from it. For example, a magistrate may decide there is no probable cause to believe the suspect committed a crime. The grand jury may refuse to indict. The prosecutor may decide not to prosecute, either because he does not think he can win or for any number of other reasons within his discretion. The petit (or trial) jury may acquit. The appellate court may reverse. Or the suspect may go the full route and serve a lengthy sentence before he is released.

Before conviction, and even after it, a suspect may be entitled to bail. The Eighth Amendment prohibits excessive bail.[5] Many state constitutions contain a similar prohibition. The

[5] See rule 18. This rule does not yet apply to the states.

theory behind the bail system is that a person charged with a crime may put up a certain amount of money, to assure his appearance at trial. This sum will be forfeited if he does not appear. The amount of bail is supposed to be just enough to assure that the suspect will not "skip." A suspect's prior record, the seriousness of the crime, his personal wealth, and his roots in the community are all considered. The bail system is intended to mirror the presumption of innocence—since all suspects are presumed innocent until proved guilty, they should not have to spend the time prior to trial in jail.

This is the theory. The practice is often opposite. If a judge determines that a suspect should not be released prior to trial, he will set bail at a prohibitive amount. If he determines that pretrial release will be safe, bail will likely be nominal. Recently there have been proposals for preventive detention, that is, confinement without a right to bail. Opponents of this plan claim it will violate the Eighth Amendment's guarantee of bail. The issue is somewhat academic because, in effect, we do not now have a system where there is a real right to bail.

In 1966, the Congress passed and the President signed the Bail Reform Act. This Act favors pretrial release and lists the factors that a federal judge can consider in coming to a decision. In addition, this Act permits suspects to be their own bail bondsmen. Traditionally, when a suspect is required to put up, say, $5,000 in bail, he will secure the services of a bail bondsman. The bondsman will guarantee the suspect's presence at trial and will be responsible to the Court for the $5,000 bail if the suspect does not appear. For his service, the bondsman receives a percentage of the total bail—usually 5 to 10 percent. The "loan" generally remains outstanding less than a year.[6] Obviously, then, the bail bondsman makes a good living. In addition, he usually protects himself by requiring friends

---

[6] It is actually not a loan because the bondsman need not put up the $5,000 until the suspect skips.

and relatives of the suspect to pledge property to him should
the suspect disappear.

The 1966 Bail Reform Act permits federal judges to allow
the suspect himself to pay only 10 percent of his total bail
into court. If the suspect fails to appear at trial, he will be
liable for the remaining 90 percent. In addition, he will be
guilty of bail jumping, an offense that carries a five year sentence.

While the Bail Reform Act has made the bail system somewhat more equitable and has reduced some of the unfairness
that the bail system works against the poor, its reforms still
operate within a structure whose very premises are subject to
question. Furthermore, the Act only applies in federal courts;
few states have as enlightened attitudes. In 1967, the President's Commission on Law Enforcement and Administration of
Justice reported:

Although bail is recognized in the law solely as a method of in-
suring the defendant's appearance at trial, judges often use it as a
way of keeping in jail persons they fear will commit crimes if released before trial. In addition to its being of dubious legality, this
procedure is ineffective in many instances. Professional criminals or
members of organized criminal syndicates have little difficulty in
posting bail, although, since crime is their way of life, they are
clearly dangerous.

If a satisfactory solution could be found to the problem of the
relatively small percentage of defendants who present a significant
risk of flight or criminal conduct before trial, the Commission
would be prepared to recommend that money bail be totally dis-
carded. Finding that solution is not easy. . . .

A partial solution for the problem would be to provide an
accelerated trial process for presumably high-risk defendants. . . .

In any case, money bail should be imposed only when reasonable
alternatives are not available. This presupposes an information-
gathering technique that can promptly provide a magistrate with
an array of facts about a defendant's history, circumstances, problems, and way of life. . . .

There are no major Supreme Court cases in this area, but the problem is drawing much attention and the Court may soon have to deal with it.[7]

What if a person goes through the process just described and at some point in it, he is denied a constitutionally guaranteed right? Since the Constitution is the supreme law of the land, a person imprisoned in violation of its demands must be released. But how does this actually happen? How do the rules discussed in this chapter operate to safeguard an individual's constitutional rights?

Assume the laws of State ABC give its policemen the power to search anyone on the street whom they believe, for any reason at all or for no reason, to be carrying a concealed weapon. A policeman, under the authority of this law, randomly searches twenty men and discovers a concealed gun. The man is tried and the prosecutor seeks to enter the gun and the policeman's testimony in evidence. The trial judge must exclude the evidence. It is immaterial that the state law authorized the policeman's conduct. The Constitution forbids it and the state law cannot override the Constitution.

If the evidence is erroneously admitted and the man is convicted and sent to jail, he can appeal to the state appellate courts. But suppose the highest state court affirms the trial judge and the Supreme Court declines to review the case. Has the man lost his right not to be convicted on the basis of illegally seized evidence because the courts have erred?

No. There is a procedure, habeas corpus, which persons in this predicament can use. "Habeas corpus" literally means "you have the body." Throughout Anglo-American legal history it has traditionally been used to test, in a court of law, the legality of a prisoner's incarceration. The writ of habeas corpus is usually addressed to the warden of the prison holding the

[7] See Ronald Goldfarb, *Ransom* (New York: Harper & Row, 1965), for a complete discussion of bail.

person who has petitioned for the writ. It orders the warden to deliver the petitioner's body to the court so that the legality of his detention can be determined. All states and the federal government provide such procedures, although sometimes the name is changed (for example, "postconviction relief," or "motion to vacate sentence"). The function is always the same—to test the legality of confinement. In fact, the writ is also used when the petitioner is not confined in the traditional sense. A person may test his induction into the armed forces through habeas corpus. A convicted person who is on probation or parole may test the legality of either status through habeas corpus.

A person confined in a federal prison, or an inmate of a state institution, may attack his confinement in a federal court through habeas corpus or an equivalent remedy.[8] When a state prisoner goes into a federal court he can claim that his confinement violates either the federal Constitution or a federal statute. In this way, the federal courts review state activity and can determine whether a state conviction violates federal statutory or constitutional law. Thus, our hypothetical prisoner, convicted on illegally seized evidence, will eventually be able to test his state conviction in a federal court through habeas corpus.

Inevitably the question is asked: what if the federal court errs? The simple answer is that the petitioner may appeal to an appellate federal court and finally to the Supreme Court. What if the Supreme Court errs? The answer is that it cannot, by definition. Since it has the final word on the meaning of the Constitution, if it determines the petitioner's rights were not violated and that the state conviction is legal, then the conviction is legal for that reason alone. Paraphrasing Justice Robert Jackson, the Supreme Court is right because it is final, it is not final because it is right.

---

[8] Rule 1 says, except in certain instances, the right of habeas corpus may not be suspended.

3

THE MEANING

OF

DUE PROCESS

Chapter 2 illustrated the importance of the four words "due process of law" in the overall operation of a Federalist criminal system. While these words have a legal meaning, they also have a political one. Indeed, since law is ultimately a result of political forces, the evolution of "due process of law" necessarily reflects the nation's political development. So, where the Court once used due process to control only the most flagrant abuses in state criminal proceedings, today, as we shall see, the phrase incorporates almost all of the safeguards in the first eight amendments. Finally, in considering the development that follows, remember that the Fifth Amendment's Due Process Clause *supplements* the protections afforded by other amendments, but the Fourteenth Amendment's Due Process Clause supplements nothing and is itself the major instrument for federal judicial control of state criminal procedure. Predictably, it is in the context of the Fourteenth Amendment that the question of definition more frequently arises.

We begin with the Supreme Court's landmark decision in *Palko* v. *Connecticut*, 302 U.S. 319 (1937). Frank Palko was charged with first degree murder, punishable by death. A jury convicted him of second degree murder and he was sentenced to life. The State appealed, claiming the trial judge made certain errors prejudicial to the case. The appellate court agreed and at his second trial Palko was convicted of first degree murder and sentenced to death.

Palko sought Supreme Court review. He argued that the Fifth Amendment's grant of immunity from double jeopardy (rule 8) would have prevented the federal government from retrying him. Likewise, the State of Connecticut denied him due process of law when it retried him.

Does due process require that a state refrain from twice putting a person in jeopardy of losing his life? The Court said no. Justice Benjamin Cardozo explained that not all the limits on the exercise of federal power apply to the states, but only those that are "of the very essence of a scheme of ordered liberty" and without which, a "fair and enlightened system of justice would be impossible." For example, the Court said freedom of thought and speech was "the matrix, the indispensable condition, of nearly every other form of freedom" and therefore, "it has come about that the domain of liberty withdrawn by the Fourteenth Amendment from encroachment by the state, has been enlarged . . . to include liberty of action." Also "fundamental [to] the concept of due process . . . is the thought that condemnation shall be rendered only after trial. . . . The hearing, moreover, must be a real one, not a sham or a pretense. . . ." But freedom from double jeopardy was not necessary to a scheme of ordered liberty; said Justice Cardozo:

Is that kind of double jeopardy to which the statute has subjected [Palko] to hardship so acute and shocking that our polity will not endure it? Does it violate those "fundamental principles of liberty and justice which lie at the base of all our civil and political institutions"? . . . The answer surely must be "no." What the answer would have to be if the state were permitted after a trial free from error to try the accused over again or to bring another case against him, we have no occasion to consider. We deal with the statute before us and no other. The state is not attempting to wear the accused out by a multitude of cases with accumulated trials. It asks no more than this, that the case against him shall go on until there shall be a trial free from the corrosion of substantial legal error . . . This is not cruelty at all, nor even vexation in any immoderate degree. If the trial had been infected with error adverse to the accused, there might have been review at his instance, and as often as necessary to purge the vicious taint. A reciprocal privilege . . . has now been granted to the State. There is here no seismic innovation. The edifice of justice stands, its symmetry, to many, greater than before.

That which is necessary to a scheme of ordered liberty has changed since 1937; despite the eloquence of Justice Cardozo, immunity from double jeopardy has recently become part of due process, in *Benton* v. *Maryland,* 395 U.S. 784 (1969). And although, in a sense, the theory of *Palko* remains—due process still refers to "fundamental principles of liberty and justice"—the Court now quotes the passage of *Palko* that speaks of "privileges and immunities . . . taken over from . . . the Federal Bill of Rights and brought within the Fourteenth Amendment by a process of absorption."[1]

"Ordered liberty" and the other slogans in *Palko* are as vague as "due process." The phrase tells us little of the Court's reasons for its holding. We can conclude that in 1937 the Court did not feel that the right Frank Palko wanted was important enough for the federal government to force its application on the states. The Court's interpretation of due process, then and now, is a reflection of the social and political attitudes of the times.

[1] Justice Harlan claims the Court is quoting this language out of context:

It is apparent that Mr. Justice Cardozo's metaphor of "absorption" was *not* intended to suggest the transplantation of case law surrounding the specifics of the first eight Amendments to the very different soil of the Fourteenth Amendment's Due Process Clause. For, as he made perfectly plain, what the Fourteenth Amendment requires of the States does not basically depend on what the first eight Amendments require of the Federal Government.

The holding in *Adamson* v. *California*, 332 U.S. 46 (1947), has also been overruled, but the case is important in the development of the concept of due process. Adamson was sentenced to death in California after a jury convicted him of murder. At his trial, the judge and prosecutor commented to the jury on Adamson's failure to take the witness stand and explain or deny evidence against him. Adamson argued that this power to comment forced him to testify, thereby violating his privilege against self-incrimination, which allowed him to refuse to testify.

The Court assumed that the power to comment did conflict with the privilege against self-incrimination; but this *Fifth* Amendment privilege limited the federal government, not the states. Nor was this privilege part of *Fourteenth* Amendment due process; it was not "implicit in the concept of ordered liberty." Ten years after *Palko*, the Court reaffirmed the theory of that case, but this time only a bare majority of five agreed.

Adamson is most important for the ideological difference reflected in the concurring opinion of Justice Felix Frankfurter and the dissenting opinions of Justices Hugo Black and Frank Murphy.

Justice Black agreed that the first eight amendments originally applied only to federal action. He argued, however, that the Fourteenth Amendment was intended to "make the Bill of Rights applicable to the states." But Justice Black realized that *Adamson* only required the Court to determine whether the privilege against self-incrimination—not the entire Bill of Rights—applied to the states. He was willing to follow the "selective process of the *Palko* decision" and to conclude that the "full protection of the Fifth Amendment's proscription against compelled testimony must be afforded by California."

Justice Frankfurter challenged Justice Black's reading of the Fourteenth Amendment. He denied that the words "due process of law" were a shorthand way of referring to all the provisions of the Bill of Rights. He noted that of the forty-three men who served on the Court since the Amendment became law, only one believed it "was a shorthand summary of the first eight Amendments." "The short answer to the suggestion that" the Due Process Clause is a way of saying that the states are obligated to adhere to the entire Bill of Rights "is that it is a strange way of saying it. It would be extraordinarily strange for a Constitution to convey such specific commands in such a roundabout and inexplicit way." And, with perhaps over-powering logic, Justice Frankfurter asked why, if due process is meant to refer to the entire Bill of Rights, does the Bill of Rights itself contain a due process clause.

Justice Frankfurter also rejected the "selective process" that Justice Black was willing to settle for. Some amendments "are in and some are out, but we are left in the dark as to which are in and which are out," Justice Frankfurter said. "If the basis of selection is merely that those provisions of the first eight Amendments are incorporated which commend themselves to individual justices as indispensable to the dignity and happi-ness of a free man, we are thrown back to a merely subjective test."

What was Justice Frankfurter's substitute for a "merely sub-jective test?" He preferred the *Palko* approach, which he read as requiring certain minimal standards which are "of the very essence of a scheme of ordered liberty." He did not see due process as frozen to the particular safeguards of the Bill of Rights. "A construction which gives to due process no inde-pendent function but turns it into a summary of the specific provisions of the Bill of Rights would . . . deprive the States of opportunity for reforms in legal process designed for extend-ing the area of freedom."

But what is "ordered liberty?" Justice Frankfurter viewed this concept in terms of natural law. "In the history of thought," he said, " 'natural law' has a much longer and much better founded meaning and justification than such subjective selec-tion of the first eight Amendments for incorporation into the

Fourteenth." In other words, due process had nothing to do with the specific guarantees of the Bill of Rights; rather, it prohibited certain state proceedings that "offend those canons of decency and fairness which express the notions of justice of English-speaking peoples even toward those charged with the most heinous offenses." And, responding to the argument that his interpretation required as much subjective judgment as Justice Black's, Justice Frankfurter said: "The judicial judgment in applying the Due Process Clause . . . is not to be based upon the idiosyncracies of a merely personal judgment." But does merely saying this make an analysis in terms of Justice Frankfurter's approach any less subjective?

Justice Black argued that the phrase "natural law" gave the Court too much power to "periodically . . . expand and contract constitutional standards to conform to the Court's conception of what at a particular time constitutes 'civilized decency' and 'fundamental principles of liberty and justice.' "

Justice Murphy had a slightly different view. He agreed with Justice Black that the Fourteenth Amendment was intended to incorporate the entire Bill of Rights, but he also agreed with Justice Frankfurter that due process should remain flexible and that it should not be limited to a single meaning. "Occasions may arise," he wrote, "where a proceeding falls so far short of conforming to fundamental standards of procedure as to warrant constitutional condemnation in terms of a lack of due process despite the absence of a specific provision in the Bill of Rights."

Whether one adopts: (1) a "natural law" and "ordered liberty" approach; (2) a "selective process" of incorporating particular amendments into due process; (3) a total incorporation of the entire Bill of Rights into the Fourteenth Amendment; or (4) either (2) or (3) plus the view that due process has an additional meaning independent of the provisions of the Bill of Rights, the judicial process of defining the criminal process is going to involve a large dose of subjective judgment. The first eight amendments, though perhaps more concrete than "ordered liberty," are necessarily vague. After all, what is "cruel and unusual punishment" or an "unreasonable search?"

The Frankfurter-Black debate recurred several times in the next dozen years. We need not review each case, but one, *Rochin* v. *California,* 342 U.S. 165 (1952), is particularly enlightening. The facts are a bit extreme. The police broke into Rochin's house, then into his bedroom. When he saw them, he quickly swallowed two capsules on his night table. The police tried to force Rochin's mouth open and when that failed, they brought him to a hospital and pumped his stomach. The two capsules emerged, and they were found to contain morphine. Rochin was convicted of illegal possession. The search was clearly unconstitutional, but the question for the Supreme Court was whether the Constitution required the state court to exclude the illegally seized capsules from introduction at trial.

Justice Frankfurter, writing the Court's opinion, defended the "ordered liberty" approach to due process. He acknowledged that this approach is "vague" but he objected to deriding it as a "resort to a revival of 'natural law.' " He said the members of the Court should "not draw on our merely personal private notions" in defining due process, but must be mindful of limits "derived from considerations that are fused in the whole nature of our judicial process." It is not enough that a judge happens to feel a particular state action is unwise; in order to declare it a violation of due process, he must believe it violates guarantees "so rooted in the traditions and conscience of our people as to be ranked as fundamental." This is a hard distinction to make at times, but the ability to make the distinction is a quality "society has a right to expect from those entrusted with ultimate judicial power."

Applying this approach, Justice Frankfurter said that the "proceedings by which this conviction was obtained do more than offend some fastidious squeamishness or private sentimentalism about combatting crime too energetically. This is conduct that shocks the conscience." It is conduct that "is bound to offend even hardened sensibilities." It therefore violated due process and the evidence should have been excluded.

Justice Black, concurring, could not accept a standard which required judges to decide if certain conduct "shocks the conscience" generally, but not their own consciences in particular. He preferred to view due process in terms of the more definite Bill of Rights.[2]

As late as 1961, *Cohen* v. *Hurley,* 366 U.S. 117 (1961), reasserted the view that any overlap between due process and the Bill of Rights guarantees was purely coincidental. But the *Palko* approach was moribund. A bare majority of the Court supported it and, in a long dissent, Justice William Brennan rejected it. In 1963, Justice Arthur Goldberg replaced an ailing Justice Frankfurter and in 1964, a new, though bare, majority changed the meaning of due process—or at least marked the beginning of a change—in *Malloy* v. *Hogan,* 378 U.S. 1 (1964).

The Superior Court of Hartford County, Connecticut, as part of an investigation into gambling, ordered Malloy to answer certain questions. Malloy refused, claiming the answers might incriminate him. He was held in contempt and sent to prison until he agreed to comply. Malloy sought release through habeas corpus, contending that Connecticut had denied him due process of law. The State argued that due process did not require a privilege against self-incrimination. The case eventually reached the Supreme Court, which held that: (1) due process included the privilege against self-incrimination (rule 9); (2) *the source of the privilege was the Fifth Amendment;*

[2] Two years later, the Court decided that an illegal police eavesdrop did not shock the conscience sufficiently to require exclusion of the overheard conversations. *Ironically, Justice Frankfurter's judicial conscience was shocked and he dissented. Irvine* v. *California,* 347 U.S. 128 (1954). *Rochin* and *Irvine* have both been superseded by *Mapp* v. *Ohio,* discussed in Chapter 4.

and (3) the states were limited by the privilege as stringently as was the federal government.

Justice Brennan, who wrote the Court's opinion, never used the words "selective incorporation," but those words accurately describe the Court's action. (Other cases have also adopted a selective incorporation approach without so naming it. Dissents and concurrences are more realistic.)

Said Justice Brennan: "The Fourteenth Amendment secures against state invasion the same privilege that the Fifth Amendment guarantees against federal infringement—the right of a person to remain silent unless he chooses to speak in the unfettered exercise of his own will, and to suffer no penalty . . . for such silence."

Justice Brennan indicated that the "shock the conscience" test was out. "The constitutional inquiry is not whether the conduct of state officers in obtaining the confession was shocking, but whether the confession is 'free and voluntary: that is, [it] must not be extracted by any sort of threats or violence, nor obtained by any direct or implied promises, however slight, nor by the exertion of any improper influence . . . .' "

Connecticut argued that even if the Fifth Amendment privilege was part of Fourteenth Amendment due process, "the availability of the federal privilege to a witness in a state inquiry is to be determined according to a less stringent standard than is applicable in a federal proceeding." This may be called the "watered-down v. full-strength" question of incorporation. The *Malloy* Court chose full-strength incorporation.

The Court has rejected the notion that the Fourteenth Amendment applies to the states only a "watered-down, subjective version of the individual guarantees of the Bill of Rights." . . . What is accorded is a privilege of refusing to incriminate one's self, and the feared prosecution may be by either federal or state authorities. . . . It would be incongruous to have different standards determine the validity of a claim of privilege based on the same feared prosecution, depending on whether the claim was asserted in a state or federal court. Therefore, the same standards must determine whether an accused's silence in either a federal or state proceeding is justified.

This language is broad enough to require full-strength application not only of the particular safeguard involved in *Malloy*, but of all future ones as well.

The Court then considered when a person may assert the privilege in response to a question. The test, said the Court, is whether the answer will incriminate, or tend to incriminate, the subject. One can certainly refuse to answer the question, "Did you kill Tom Smith?" But one can also refuse, without penalty, to answer such simple questions as, "Do you know Jack Jones?" or "Have you ever been to Los Angeles?" Answers to these questions could conceivably provide a link in a chain of evidence proving guilt of a particular crime.[3]

Justice John Harlan dissented.

I can only read the Court's opinion as accepting in fact what it rejects in theory: the application to the States, via the Fourteenth Amendment, of the forms of federal criminal procedure embodied within the first eight Amendments to the Constitution. . . . [T]he logical gap between the Court's premises and its novel constitutional conclusion can, I submit, be bridged only by the additional premise that the Due Process Clause of the Fourteenth Amendment is a shorthand directive to this Court to pick and choose among the provisions of the first eight Amendments and apply those chosen, freighted with their entire accompanying body of federal doctrine, to law enforcement in the States.

[3] An answer to a particular question may cause the speaker to waive his privilege against self-incrimination. Therefore, an individual may cautiously refuse to answer even those questions that could not incriminate him. This is why we occasionally learn that someone has taken the "Fifth" hundreds of times. It is not that an answer to each and every question asked will incriminate the subject, but that an answer to any question may waive the right to refuse to answer a subsequent one. It is difficult to justify this rule. It discourages cooperation with investigatory bodies. Lately, courts have begun to realize this. See, for example, *Shendal* v. *United States*, 312 F.2d 564 (1963).

Justice Harlan agreed that the meaning of due process should be subject to constant reexamination, and that this reexamination should always consider the guarantees of the Bill of Rights. He did not believe, however, that the judicial function should be "short-circuited by the simple device of incorporating into due process, without critical examination, the whole body of law which surrounds a specific prohibition directed against the Federal government."

The consequence of such an approach to due process as it pertains to the States is inevitably disregard of all relevant differences which may exist between state and federal criminal law and its enforcement. The ultimate result is compelled uniformity, which is inconsistent with the purpose of our federal system and which is achieved either by encroachment on the States' sovereign powers or by dilution in federal law enforcement of the specific protections found in the Bill of Rights.

Justice Harlan applied the fundamental fairness test and concluded that Connecticut's rule satisfied that test.

Justice Harlan's argument is powerful. Whether it is persuasive ultimately depends on one's political and social values, as well as legal and historical considerations. If each of our fifty states were as solicitous of the rights of the individual as some states are, the need for national protection of these rights might be less and, therefore, Justice Harlan's approach to federalism preferable.

It can also be argued in response to Justice Harlan that the "relevant differences . . . between state and federal criminal law" do not justify official conduct that falls below the guarantees in the Bill of Rights. The Court does not ignore these differences when it applies a safeguard from the first eight Amendments to the states. Rather, it says that the importance of the safeguard makes the differences irrelevant.[4]

---

[4] A year after *Malloy,* the Court overruled *Adamson* v. *California* in *Griffin* v. *California,* 380 U.S. 609 (1965). *Griffin* holds that it is a vio-

In *Pointer* v. *Texas,* 380 U.S. 400 (1965), the Supreme Court held that the Sixth Amendment's guarantee that a defendant shall "be confronted with the witnesses against him" (rule 15) applied, through the Fourteenth Amendment, to the states.

Pointer was arrested for the armed robbery of Phillips. He was taken before a state judge for a preliminary hearing in order to determine whether there was sufficient evidence to hold him for trial. At the hearing, Phillips said Pointer had robbed him at gunpoint. Pointer did not have a lawyer and made feeble attempts to cross-examine Phillips himself. Subsequently, Pointer was indicted and tried. Since in the interim Phillips had moved away from the area and was not available to testify at the trial, the prosecutor offered the transcript of his testimony at the preliminary hearing. Pointer was convicted and his case eventually reached the Supreme Court.

The Court said: (1) The "right of cross-examination is included in the right of an accused in a criminal case to confront the witnesses against him." This decision was necessary because the Sixth Amendment says nothing about cross-examination, only confrontation (rule 15). (2) "[T]he right of confrontation and cross-examination is an essential and fundamental requirement for the kind of fair trial which is this country's constitutional goal." (3) A defendant is "entitled to be tried in accordance with the protection of the confrontation guarantee of the Sixth Amendment, and that . . . guarantee, like the right against compelled self-incrimination, is 'to be enforced against the states under the Fourteenth Amendment according to the same standards that protect those personal rights against federal encroachment.' "

The Court held that Pointer had been denied his confrontation right. Phillips' absence from the trial did not automatically

---

lation of an accused's due process privilege against self-incrimination to comment to the jury on a defendant's failure to take the witness stand.

lead to this result. "The case before us," said the Court, "would be quite a different one had Phillips' statement been taken at a fullfledged hearing at which [Pointer] had been represented by counsel who had been given a complete and adequate opportunity to cross-examine." Since Phillips' statement "had not been taken at a time and under circumstances affording petitioner through counsel an adequate opportunity to cross-examine Phillips," it could not have been introduced at a federal criminal trial. And since the same standards apply "whether the [confrontation] right is denied in a federal or state proceeding, it follows that the use of the transcript to convict [Pointer] denied him a constitutional right. . . ."

Pointer is especially important in a study of the development of due process because of the concurring opinions of Justices Harlan and Goldberg.

Justice Harlan concurred in the Court's result, but not in its reasoning. "This is another step in the onward march of the long since discredited 'incorporation' doctrine . . . which for some reason that I have not yet been able to fathom has come into the sunlight in recent years." Justice Harlan determined that the state judgment had to be reversed but only "because a right of confrontation is 'implicit in the concept of ordered liberty.' " He continued:

While either of these constitutional approaches brings one to the same end result in this particular case, there is a basic difference between the two in the kind of future constitutional development they portend. The concept of Fourteenth Amendment due process embodied in *Palko* and a host of other thoughtful past decisions now rapidly falling into discard, recognizes that our Constitution tolerates, indeed encourages, differences between the methods used to effectuate legitimate federal and state concerns, subject to the requirements of fundamental fairness "implicit in the concept of ordered liberty." The philosophy of "incorporation," on the other hand, subordinates all such state differences to the particular requirements of the Federal Bill of Rights . . . and increasingly subjects state legal processes to enveloping federal

judicial authority. "Selective" incorporation or "absorption"
amounts to little more than a diluted form of the full incorporation
theory. Whereas it rejects full incorporation because of recognition
that not all of the guarantees of the Bill of Rights should be deemed
"fundamental," it at the same time ignores the possibility that not
all phases of any given guaranty described in the Bill of Rights are
necessarily fundmental.

Justice Goldberg agreed with both the reasoning and the result of the Court. In a concurrence, he discussed selective incorporation and Justice Harlan's objections to it.

. . . Since I was not on the Court when the incorporation issue
was joined . . . I deem it appropriate to set forth briefly my view
on this subject. . . .
I cannot agree that this [selective incorporation] process has
"come into the sunlight in recent years." Rather I believe that it has
its origins at least as far back as *Twining* v. *New Jersey*, 211 U.S.
78, 99, where the Court stated that "it is possible that some of the
personal rights safeguarded by the first eight Amendments against
National action may also be safeguarded against state action, because
a denial of them would be a denial of due process of law. . . ."
Furthermore, I do not agree . . . that once a provision of the
Bill of Rights has been held applicable to the States by the Fourteenth Amendment, it does not apply to the States in full strength.
Such a view would have the Fourteenth Amendment apply to the
States only a "watered-down, subjective version of the individual
guarantees of the Bill of Rights. . . ." It would allow the States
greater latitude than the Federal Government to abridge concededly
fundamental liberties protected by the Constitution. While I quite
agree with Mr. Justice Brandeis that "[i]t is one of the happy inci-
dents of the federal system that a . . . State may . . . serve as a
laboratory; and try novel social and economic experiments" . . . I do
not believe that this includes the power to experiment with the fundamental liberties of citizens safeguarded by the Bill of Rights. . . .
Finally, I do not see that my Brother HARLAN's view would
further any legitimate interests of federalism. It would require this
Court to intervene in the state judicial process with considerable
lack of predictability and with a consequent likelihood of considerable friction. . . . And, to deny to the states the power to impair a
fundamental constitutional right is not to increase federal power

but, rather, to limit the power of both federal and state governments in favor of safeguarding the fundamental rights and liberties of the individual. In my view this promotes rather than undermines the basic policy of avoiding excess concentration of power in government, federal or state, which underlines our concepts of federalism.

In *Duncan* v. *Louisiana,* 391 U.S. 145 (1968), the last major case in the development of due process, the Court applied the Sixth Amendment's right to trial by jury in criminal cases to the states. Under the "full-strength" rule, this would mean that all criminal trials must be to juries of twelve and that the verdict must be unanimous. However, the *Duncan* Court hinted that the traditional definition of "trial by jury" was flexible. Indeed, two years after *Duncan,* in *Williams* v. *Florida,* 399 U.S. 78 (1970), the Court held that six-man juries satisfied the constitutional requirement of jury trial. There was no magic in the number twelve.

The constitutional guarantee of trial by jury does not extend to cases in which a defendant is charged with a petty offense. The term "petty offense" is vague, but the Court has determined that a jury trial is necessary—and an offense is no longer petty—when the possible punishment can exceed six months in jail. *Baldwin* v. *New York,* 399 U.S. 66 (1970).

Time will further define the boundaries of the right to jury trial. Our point is that the Court has applied to the states the same Sixth Amendment guarantee that applies to the federal government.

Duncan is a microcosm of our entire discussion of due process. The majority opinion, written by Justice Byron White, relies on selective incorporation and briefly reviews the Court's varying approaches to the problem. Justice Black's concurrence recalls his *Adamson* dissent and discusses his current view. Justice Abe Fortas agrees that due process should include the right to trial by jury, but he questions whether the states should have to obey "all the ancillary rules" incidental to trial in federal courts. This is the "full-strength v. watered-down" issue. Justice Harlan reviews his (and Justice Frankfurter's) view and concludes that fundamental fairness leads him to a result different from the Court's. Excerpts from Justice White's opinion follow:

The Fourteenth Amendment denies the States the power to "deprive any person of life, liberty, or property, without due process of law." In resolving conflicting claims concerning the meaning of this spacious language, the Court has looked increasingly to the Bill of Rights for guidance; many of the rights guaranteed by the first eight Amendments to the Constitution have been held to be protected against state action by the Due Process Clause of the Fourteenth Amendment. That clause now protects the right to compensation for property taken by the State; the rights of speech, press, and religion covered by the First Amendment; the Fourth Amendment rights to be free from unreasonable searches and seizures and to have excluded from criminal trials any evidence illegally seized; the right guaranteed by the Fifth Amendment to be free of compelled self-incrimination; and the Sixth Amendment rights to counsel, to a speedy and public trial, to confrontation of opposing witnesses, and to compulsory process for obtaining witnesses.

The test for determining whether a right extended by the Fifth and Sixth Amendments with respect to federal criminal proceedings is also protected against state action by the Fourteenth Amendment has been phrased in a variety of ways in the opinions of this Court. The question has been asked whether a right is among those "fundamental principles of liberty and justice which lie at the base of all our civil and political institutions," . . . whether it is "basic in our system of jurisprudence," . . . and whether it is "a fundamental right, essential to a fair trial," . . . . The claim before us is that the right to trial by jury guaranteed by the Sixth Amendment meets these tests. The position of Louisiana, on the other hand, is that the Constitution imposes upon the States no duty to give a jury trial in any criminal case, regardless of the seriousness of the crime or the size of the punishment which may be imposed. Because we believe that trial by jury in criminal cases is fundamental to the American scheme of justice, we hold that the Fourteenth Amendment guarantees a right of jury trial in all criminal cases which—were they to be tried in a federal court—would come within the Sixth Amendment's guarantee. . . .

Justice White listed the guarantees that have been incorporated into the Fourteenth Amendment's Due Process Clause. A year later, the Supreme Court applied the Fifth Amendment's requirement of immunity from double jeopardy (rule 8) to the states. *Benton* v. *Maryland.* A review of Chapter 2 will show that the following rules now bind the states: 4, 5, 6, 8, 9, 11, 12, 13, 15, 16, 17, and 20. Not binding are 7, 18, and 19. The other rules in Chapter 2 are by their nature not relevant to the problem.

Today, practically the entire Bill of Rights controls state action in the area of criminal procedure. This is not because each of these safeguards is inherently fundamental to all conceivable systems of criminal procedure, but because, as Justice White wrote in *Duncan,* each is "fundamental in the context of the criminal processes maintained by the American States."

4

ARREST, SEARCH,
AND SEIZURE

When can a policeman, as the official representative of government, arrest an individual? When can he stop him on the street? Are they the same thing? When can the policeman search? What do we mean by "arrest" and "search"? What happens if the policeman breaks the rules? These are a few of the questions this Chapter will attempt to answer in discussing the dimensions of the Fourth Amendment (rules 4–6).

I The Ground Rules

A. Protected Areas

The Fourth Amendment only protects "persons, houses, papers, and effects." What are these? The answer to this question is important because anything that is not one of these four items receives no constitutional protection—that is, it is not a protected area.

Like many other questions in the law, this one is most easily answered for items at either end of the continuum. For example, a man's house is clearly a protected area, but a public park is not. So, a policeman, before he searches a house, must satisfy the Fourth Amendment's demands, but he can "search" (that is, watch what happens in) the park without check.

The difficult problems are posed by areas that are more enclosed than the park, but less than the house. Thus, is a tent pitched in a public park protected? Since there is a myriad of situations that can exist in this area, the best one can do is try to induce the underlying rationale from a consideration of the places that have been held either protected or unprotected.

Supreme Court cases have placed the following areas within the Fourth Amendment's protection: a business office, a store, an automobile, a hotel room, an apartment, a taxi. Lower courts have held hospital rooms, school lockers, and an employee's unlocked desk protected areas. On the other hand, there is nothing to stop a policeman, or anyone else, from looking through an open door or window. He may view the inside of a parked car with a flashlight. And the visiting room at a jail has been held unprotected.

Perhaps the most interesting site to come up for court review is the public bathroom. When authorities at a national park had reason to believe that a certain men's room was being used for homosexual purposes, the police placed themselves in an attic just above the stalls. From 11 P.M. on, they observed the comings and goings in the three stalls below. Some forty legitimate users were viewed before the defendants were observed committing homosexual acts in violation of the law. A federal court of appeals upheld the conviction. The majority did not believe public toilets came within the full protection of the Fourth Amendment. Though the police could not engage in such practices whenever they wished, if there was probable cause to believe the toilets were being used for illegal practices, continuous observation was held permissible although there was no probable cause to suspect any particular occupant.

Other cases, also involving public toilets, have produced a different result. Perhaps public toilets have finally been brought within the Fourth Amendment's protection as a result of *Katz* v. *United States,* discussed in the next Chapter. That case protected telephone conversations in a public booth because the person using the phone reasonably expected that his conversations were private. Not only the nature of the place but also the reasonableness of the occupant's expectation of privacy must be considered. A person using a public bathroom reasonably expects privacy.

Perhaps, then, that is the rule we can draw from the cases. A place is a protected area if, considering the nature of the place, the user reasonably believes he is free from visual and aural interception.

B. Protection From What?

Once there is a protected area, what is it protected from? The Fourth Amendment merely speaks of the "right of the people to be secure" and says this right shall not be "violated" except under certain circumstances. The strong implication, supported by the historical context, is that the Fourth Amendment protects against official, that is, state, action. But what about *private* searches of a protected area? What if, for example, your landlord searches your closets, or a co-worker searches your desk, in a way that would violate the Fourth Amendment if done by a policeman? He discovers evidence of a crime, turns it over to the authorities, and you are eventually prosecuted and convicted on the basis of that evidence. Has there been a violation of your Fourth Amendment rights? No. This is a new area, and the answer may change to yes, with time, and perhaps it should. The result is inconsistent with the other rules in this area for two reasons: (1) it is no less an invasion of a person's privacy when the invader is a policeman than when he is a private citizen; (2) the court, by admitting the evidence, lends to the invasion the element of state involvement necessary (if it is necessary) to bring the Fourth Amendment into play.

There is one exception. If a private person is solicited by the state to search a protected area, his action becomes state action and the Fourth Amendment applies.

C. Search Warrants

Unless there is an exception permitting a warrantless search, a policeman must secure a warrant before he can search an individual. According to the second part of the Fourth Amendment,

no Warrants shall issue but upon probable cause, supported by Oath or affirmation, and particularly describing the place to be searched, and the persons or things to be seized.

In order to secure a warrant, then, the policeman must swear or affirm the existence of certain facts equaling "probable cause" to justify a search. The key is "probable cause." It is needed not only to get a warrant, but also, in most cases, when a search is conducted under an exception to the warrant requirement.

What is "probable cause"? Is it another one of those vague phrases, like "due process" or "ordered liberty"? Clearly it is. We shall later discuss cases that attempt to define it in terms of their particular facts. But in this area, each case is individual, and whatever meaning "probable cause" has today may not carry over to tomorrow. We can state, however, that "probable" cause means something more than "possible" cause (suspicion) and something less than "absolute" cause (certainty). It is, essentially, an attempt to articulate the balance between two countervailing societal interests: detection of criminal activity and security from state intrusion into the privacy of innocent persons. Thus, as reliable information of criminal activity increases, our reluctance to permit a search decreases. "Probable cause" is the point at which the balance tips in favor of the search.

Once the policeman has probable cause to suspect criminal activity, and there is no exception permitting a warrantless search, how does he get a warrant? The process is fairly simple. He takes his facts to a magistrate (a judicial officer), swears (or affirms) that the facts are true, or that he believes them to be true, and states the source of his information. If the magistrate believes the facts show probable cause, and that, considering their source, their veracity can be credited, a warrant will issue "particularly describing the place to be searched, and the persons or things to be seized." The policeman, without unnecessary delay, since the facts can change, then executes the warrant by conducting the search. Generally, after the search is concluded, the policeman will file a report stating the results.

Assuming a policeman will be able to get a warrant anyway, why not let him search? Isn't it just as easy to review a policeman's decision that he had probable cause as to review the decision of the magistrate who issues the warrant? Of course. The reason, in theory, that a warrant is preferred is that we do not want the policeman making the decision, but a magistrate who we like to believe is disinterested, that is, not as eager to solve crimes at the expense of people's rights. This is the theory. Sometimes, however, courts review only whether the policeman acted with probable cause when he searched. They do not ask the second question: should the policeman have asked for a warrant and let the magistrate make the decision whether there was probable cause to search.

D. Warrantless Searches

The area of warrantless searches makes the rules governing search warrants seem like child's play. No doubt more searches are conducted under one or another of the exceptions to the general rule than pursuant to a warrant. It is, therefore, important to understand the dimensions of each exception.

1. CONSENT

The first exception is consent. The police do not need a search warrant or any other justification to search (even probable cause) when there is consent to the search. But what is consent? Who can give it and when is it given?

In *Stoner* v. *California,* 376 U.S. 483 (1964), the police searched a man's hotel room after the room clerk let them enter in the man's absence. The Court said there was no valid consent by the man to the search. The room clerk, along with maids and repairmen, may have the right to enter a guest's room, but they have no right to enter for the purpose of allowing a police search.

"It is important to bear in mind that it was the petitioner's constitutional right which was at stake here," said the eight–man majority, "and not the night clerk's or the hotel's. It was a right, therefore, which only the petitioner could waive by word or deed, either directly or through an agent."

In *McDonald* v. *United States,* 335 U.S. 451 (1948), the Court applied the same rule to a boarding house guest, and in *Chapman* v. *United States,* 365 U.S. 610 (1961), the search of a house, occupied by a tenant, violated the tenant's constitutional right even though the search was authorized by the landlord.

In *Bumper* v. *North Carolina,* 391 U.S. 543 (1968), the police went to a suspect's home, owned by his grandmother, and told the grandmother they had a search warrant. She let them search and they discovered evidence which was later offered in a criminal proceeding against the suspect. The State argued that since the grandmother consented to the search, the validity of the warrant was irrelevant. The Supreme Court disagreed. True, the grandmother had consented, but the consent was not "freely and voluntarily given."

A search conducted in reliance upon a warrant cannot later be justified on the basis of consent if it turns out that the warrant was invalid. . . . When a law enforcement officer claims authority to search a home under a warrant, he announces in effect that the occupant has no right to resist the search. The situation is instinct with coercion—albeit colorably lawful coercion. Where there is coercion there cannot be consent.

Note, however, that if the grandmother had freely consented to a search of her house, her grandson could only have objected to the extent that the police entered his room. The grandmother could consent to a search of any common areas over which she had dominion, notwithstanding the fact that her grandson also lived in them.

2. BORDER SEARCHES

Another exception to the general rule is border searches. When a person crosses a border into the United States, customs officers search him and his baggage quite thoroughly. They can do this, and they do not even need probable cause. Merely crossing the border entitles the government to search. However, there are some limits. In a recent case in a lower federal court, a person was given a rather in-depth anal examination by a doctor under *nonhospital* conditions. The "fruits" of the search were four small capsules of narcotics. The search was held unreasonable. This does not mean such a search is not permitted. It is! It simply means it was not permitted on the particular facts of the case because of nonhospital conditions.

The rules in this area, or the absence of them, are a reflection of the belief that there is no other way to control smuggling. This may or may not be true, but even assuming it is true, certain values may be more important than the off-chance of catching someone importing contraband. One may accept the possibility of smuggling to justify a search of a traveler's suitcase on mere suspicion. But something more than a hunch—if less than probable cause—should be present before the government can conduct the rather thorough search of the traveler that frequently occurs.

3. AUTOMOBILES AND MOVING VEHICLES

A warrantless search is also permitted, as a third exception to the general rule, when a moving vehicle is involved. This does not mean the standard for searching is any less—probable cause is still needed—but the courts will not require a warrant in these cases. The reason is necessity. A moving vehicle may disappear while the policeman is off getting his warrant. However, where the vehicle is in the policeman's custody, and there is no chance of it leaving, the need created by mobility is gone and a warrant is required. So, in *Preston* v. *United States,* 376 U.S. 364 (1964), a warrantless search of an automobile locked in a police garage was held unconstitutional. There was no reason not to secure a warrant first.

4. EXIGENT CIRCUMSTANCES

This is a catch-all exception. Sometimes a court will review the facts of the case before it and hold that "exigent circumstances" justified the particular warrantless search. Probable cause is still necessary. For example, in *Warden* v. *Hayden* the police entered a house after being told that an armed robber had entered less than five minutes before. They seized weapons and incriminating clothing prior to or contemporaneous with the arrest of the robber. The Court, holding the search constitutional, said:

The Fourth Amendment does not require police officers to delay in the course of an investigation if to do so would gravely endanger their lives or the lives of others. Speed here was essential, and only a thorough search of the house for persons and weapons could have insured that Hayden was the only man present and that the police had control of all weapons which could be used against them or to effect an escape. [387 U.S. 294 (1967)]

An interesting application of the exigent circumstances exception occurred in *Schmerber* v. *California,* 384 U.S. 757 (1966), a case we shall consider again in Chapter 7. While Schmerber was being treated at a hospital after an automobile accident, the police directed the doctors, over Schmerber's objections, to take a blood sample. The sample showed a large alcohol content and Schmerber was convicted of driving while under the influence of alcohol. The blood test was challenged on Fourth Amendment, among other, grounds. A five-man majority upheld the conviction even though no warrant to "search" Schmerber's bloodstream had been secured. The proof might be eliminated from the body in the time it would take to get a warrant and so, under these "special circumstances" a warrantless search was permitted.[1]

5. SEARCHES INCIDENT TO ARRESTS

A policeman may conduct a search incident to a lawful arrest; to be lawful, an arrest requires probable cause to believe a crime has been committed and that the person arrested committed it. Thus, under this exception, too, probable cause is a prerequisite.

---

[1] The Court's insistence that its conclusion was based on the facts before it and that the "integrity of an individual's person" was a "cherished value," did not assuage the four dissenters. In addition to the dissents of Justices Warren and Black, Justice Douglas argued that Schmerber's "zone of privacy" had been violated, and Justice Fortas eloquently wrote that he did not believe the state had the right to "commit any kind of violence upon the person . . . and the extraction of blood, over protest, is an act of violence."

This exception to the rule requiring search warra̶ certain potential for abuse because the courts do n̶ a policeman with probable cause to arrest get the pri̶o̶ṛ̶ proval of a judicial officer. In other words, arrest without arrest warrants tends to be the rule, and only in exceptional circumstances will the courts require the officer to first see a magistrate.

Generally, this rule seems reasonable because an arresting policeman does not often have the opportunity to secure an arrest warrant between the time he develops probable cause to take a certain suspect into custody and the time he actually apprehends the suspect. But if it is necessary to have a warrant to search, though not if the search follows a lawful arrest, a policeman need only find a ground to arrest (and there are many if the will is present) in order to search. The search then becomes legitimate even if it would not have been legitimate before the arrest, either because there was no warrant or basis to secure a warrant. There is always the possibility that the arrest will be held invalid—in which case the whole structure will tumble down, including the search—but it is easier for a policeman to justify an arrest in retrospect than to justify a warrantless search. And if the arrest is valid, and the search turns up evidence of any crime, even if it was not the original reason for the arrest (for example, a concealed weapon or contraband), that evidence is admissible in court.

When is a person considered "under arrest" so that a warrantless search is permissible? "Arrest" has never been authoritatively defined and whether one has occurred in a particular case will ultimately depend on the facts of that case. An arrest can occur, of course, even though the officer never says "You're under arrest." At the very least, taking a person into "custody" —limiting his freedom for more than a very short time—is an arrest. Merely stopping him on the street when he is free to move on is not.

What about a summons for littering or speeding or any of the other petty offenses for which a policeman can ticket some-

one. The key words are "ticket" and "summons." If the policeman simply gives the offender a summons or "ticket" to appear
in court, without taking him into custody, there is no arrest and
the underlying reasons for permitting a search are absent. These
underlying reasons are (1) to protect the police officer from
harm if the prisoner has a concealed weapon; and (2) to keep
the prisoner from disposing of evidence he may happen to have
on his person or in his immediate control. In other words, the
circumstances demand a search after an arrest, so an exception
is created. But these circumstances are absent when a person is
given a traffic summons. And the general rule, in most jurisdictions, is that a search is not allowed as incident to, say, a speeding ticket. A ticket is not equivalent to an arrest since there is
no taking into custody; therefore, there is nothing for the search
to be incident to.[2]

If the two reasons for permitting a search incident to a lawful arrest are the protection of the policeman and the preserva-
tion of evidence, the extent to which the police are permitted
to search under this exception should be limited to the satis-
faction of those two goals. A more extensive search should be
pursuant to a warrant.

For a long time the Court was vague on this issue, jumping
from one position to the other. For example, in *Harris* v. *United
States,* 331 U.S. 145 (1947), the Court upheld a search of a
four-room apartment as incident to the arrest of a man inside
the apartment. In *United States* v. *Rabinowitz,* 339 U.S. 56
(1950), the Court approved the search of the desk and file
cabinets in a one-room office. Then, in *Preston* v. *United States,*
376 U.S. 364 (1964), the warrantless search of the suspect's
car after it had already been removed to the police garage was

---

[2] In *Terry* v. *Ohio,* discussed subsequently, the Court suggests that
there are "degrees" of arrest and that the permissible scope of the ensuing search depends on the extent to which the person of the suspect is
justifiably seized (or arrested). For the time being, we will use "arrest"
to refer to the action of the policeman in placing the suspect in official
custody and removing him to the stationhouse.

held invalid. The inconsistencies were finally resolved in *Chimel* v. *California,* where the Court strictly limited the scope of searches incident to arrests.

When an arrest is made, it is reasonable for the arresting officer to search the person arrested in order to remove any weapons that the latter might seek to use in order to resist arrest or effect his escape. Otherwise, the officer's safety might well be endangered and the arrest itself frustrated. In addition, it is entirely reasonable for the arresting officer to search for and seize any evidence on the arrestee's person in order to prevent its concealment or destruction. And the area into which an arrestee might reach in order to grab a weapon or evidentiary items must, of course, be governed by a like rule. A gun on a table or in a drawer in front of one who is arrested can be as dangerous to the arresting officer as one concealed in the clothing of the person arrested. There is ample justification, therefore, for a search of the arrestee's person and the area "within his immediate control"—construing that phrase to mean the area from within which he might gain possession of a weapon or destructible evidence.

There is no comparable justification, however, for routinely searching any room other than that in which an arrest occurs—or, for that matter, for searching through all the desk drawers or other closed or concealed areas in that room itself. Such searches, in the absence of well-recognized exceptions, may be made only under the authority of a search warrant. . . . [395 U.S. 752(1969)]

Chimel is an important case because, at least in theory and hopefully in practice, it closes one of the widest loopholes to avoidance of Fourth Amendment guarantees. Under the *Harris-Rabinowitz* approach, if the police wanted to search a man's house but had no probable cause to do so, they had only to arrest him there. So long as the arrest was supported by probable cause, the ensuing search was permissible. After *Chimel,* this is no longer true for houses. Automobiles still present a problem. The Court seems willing to permit searches of them without warrants even when the car is in official custody and there is no danger that it will be moved away. *Chambers* v. *Maroney*, 399 U.S. 42 (1970).

II   The Consequences of an Unlawful Search

The first part of this Chapter contains the ground rules governing search and seizure. An important corollary to these rules is the sanction imposed by the courts if the rules are broken. If there is no sanction, or if the sanction is ineffective, the rules become almost academic. It is interesting that for quite a long time, there was no effective sanction against official disregard of Fourth Amendment principles.

In *Weeks* v. *United States,* 232 U.S. 383 (1914), the Supreme Court held that in a federal prosecution, the Fourth Amendment required the exclusion of evidence acquired through an illegal search or seizure. In *Wolf* v. *Colorado,* 338 U.S. 25 (1949), the Court decided that freedom from unreasonable searches and seizures was also part of due process, that the Fourth Amendment applied to the states. But the six-man majority, in an opinion by Justice Frankfurter, refused to hold that the states must exclude evidence acquired illegally; the "exclusionary rule" was not part of the Fourth Amendment and so it did not apply to the states. In other words, the law enforcement agencies of the several states could not engage in unreasonable searches and seizures, but if they did, anything they found could nevertheless be used in evidence against the person whose rights were violated. The exclusionary rule was only one of several ways in which states might assure compliance with the Fourth Amendment, but the Constitution did not require it.

Justice Murphy, dissenting, said that other ways to assure compliance with the Fourth Amendment were unsatisfactory.

One alternative was to criminally prosecute errant officers; but Justice Murphy realistically rejected this possibility as highly unlikely to occur. Another alternative was to permit the person whose rights were violated to sue the offending officer in civil court. But it is doubtful whether a jury will punish a policeman for catching a criminal too industriously, and, if it does, the damages will usually be too small to affect future conduct.

After twelve years of creating exceptions to *Wolf,* and then exceptions to the exceptions (recall the *Rochin* and *Irvine* cases in Chapter Three), the Supreme Court changed its mind in 1961, when, five to four, it decided that the exclusionary rule did apply to the states. *Mapp* v. *Ohio,* 367 U.S. 643 (1961).

Justice Tom Clark, speaking for himself and three others, said: "Today we once again examine *Wolf's* constitutional documentation of the right to privacy free from unreasonable state intrusion, and, after its dozen years on our books, are led by it to close the only courtroom door remaining open to evidence secured by official lawlessness in flagrant abuse of that basic right, reserved to all persons as a specific guarantee against that very same unlawful conduct. We hold that all evidence obtained by searches and seizures in violation of the Constitution is, by that same authority, inadmissible in a state court."

Justice Clark noted that when a confession is coerced, the Fifth and Fourteenth Amendments kept it out of federal and state courts, respectively. Didn't it make sense, then, to apply the same rule "to what is tantamount to coerced testimony by way of unconstitutional seizure of goods, papers, effects, documents, etc.?" The exclusionary rule became part of the Fourth Amendment, and, therefore, part of the Fourteenth.

Only three other Justices joined in Justice Clark's opinion. A majority was achieved with a concurrence by Justice Black, who had also concurred in *Wolf.* After reconsideration, Justice Black decided that the exclusionary rule did apply to the states after all. However, he believed its application was required, not by the Fourth Amendment alone (which, he said, merely prohibits unreasonable searches), but by the Fourth and Fifth Amendments combined.

Justice Harlan, in a powerful dissent, argued that the Fifth Amendment had not yet been applied to the states (this was three years before *Malloy* v. *Hogan*) and so Justice Black's concurrence relied on reasoning that the rest of the Court had not yet accepted. In addition, Justice Harlan believed that principles of federalism required that the states be free to reject the exclusionary rule. "In my view," he said, "this Court should continue to forbear from fettering the states with an adamant rule which may embarrass them in coping with their own peculiar problems in criminal law enforcement."

The exclusionary rule, then, is the prime sanction for guaranteeing compliance with the Fourth Amendment's demands. But it is important to recognize, as Chief Justice Warren has[3], that even this powerful sanction has its limits. It is more effective in controlling decisions made after consideration than action taken under pressure. For example, if a policeman goes off to search a house without a warrant, exclusion of the evidence will possibly assure his application for a warrant next time. However, if a policeman instinctively takes certain action during, for example, a chase because he believes that action will assure capture with the least possible danger, detailed analysis of this quick decision is less likely to affect the officer's subsequent behavior. In short, the courts are more concerned with thought-out police practices—the *structure* of law enforcement—than with isolated decisions under stress.

The exclusionary rule does not only forbid introduction of the particular evidence secured in violation of the Fourth Amendment, but also other evidence to which the tainted evidence may lead. In *Silverthorne Lumber Co.* v. *United States,* 251 U.S. 385 (1920), Justice Oliver Wendell Holmes said:

---

[3] In *Terry* v. *Ohio,* discussed later.

"The essence of a provision forbidding the acquisition of evidence in a certain way is that not merely evidence so acquired shall not be used before the Court but that it shall not be used at all." In *Nardone* v. *United States,* 308 U.S. 338 (1939), Justice Frankfurter gave this idea a metaphor and it has since been known as the "fruit of the poisonous tree" doctrine. This doctrine excludes evidence secured with the help of information from an illegal search. For example, if an unlawful search of an office produces papers that contain names of potential witnesses, the witnesses will be excluded from testifying against the owner of the office even if the state can show that it might have discovered these witnesses by some independent route. Or, if an illegal search produces a key that opens a safe containing a map leading to a buried suitcase full of bills recently stolen from a bank, the key, the safe, the map, the suitcase, and the money cannot be used in evidence against the suspect who was illegally searched. In a recent California case, the State Supreme Court excluded a confession induced by showing the defendant incriminating, but illegally seized, evidence.

The state will avoid the fruit of the poisonous tree doctrine if it can show that the discovery, though an ultimate result of an illegal search, is so "attenuated" from the search that it cannot reasonably be called a "product" of the search.

We have been discussing the admissibility of evidence secured through an illegal search. What if the police make an illegal arrest—for example, one without probable cause or one without a warrant (in those few situations when an arrest warrant is required)? One consequence, as we have seen, is that evidence from the ensuing search will be excluded. But what if, as a result of an illegal arrest, the suspect voluntarily confesses? Must the confession also be excluded as the fruit of an illegal arrest? Yes, said *Wong Sun* v. *United States,* 371 U.S. 471 (1963): "Verbal evidence which derives so immediately from an unlawful entry and an unauthorized arrest as the officers' action in the present case is no less the 'fruit' of official illegality than the more common tangible fruits of the unwarranted intrusion."

If there is an illegal arrest and nothing else—no evidence or confession to suppress—the suspect has no meaningful recourse. The state can try the suspect as though his arrest were legal and, if he is convicted, the judge will sentence him. The state need not release the defendant and rearrest him properly. The policeman may be civilly liable for false arrest, but success in such actions is unlikely, particularly if there was a conviction.

III   Probable Cause

The Fourth Amendment says that "no Warrants shall issue, but upon probable cause." Probable cause is also needed for an arrest or search without a warrant, except for border searches and searches on consent. As we noted above, the concept of probable cause represents an attempt to articulate a balance between the societal interest in solving crimes and the sometimes countervailing interest of respecting individual privacy. The best way to understand the meaning of this standard is to review the cases that have considered it.

Draper v. *United States,* 358 U.S. 307 (1959), involved a warrantless arrest. Hereford, an informer, told Marsh, an FBI agent, that on the morning of September 8 or 9, a man would arrive at the Denver train terminal from Chicago, carrying heroin. Hereford, who had often given the police reliable tips, described the man in detail, including his dress and the fact that he walked fast. On September 9, a man meeting Hereford's description got off a Chicago train in Denver and Marsh arrested him, searched him, and discovered heroin. At his trial, Draper made two claims: (1) an arrest cannot be based on hearsay; (2) even if an arrest can be based on hearsay, the information here did not amount to probable cause. Hearsay, as used in the *Draper* opinion, refers to facts or evidence a person does not know to be true himself, but has been told by another. The Supreme Court rejected the first contention, holding that probable cause may be based on an informer's information, even though the policeman has no personal knowledge of the information.

The Court also held that Hereford's information, corroborated by the events at the station, amounted to probable cause. When Marsh, pursuing Hereford's tip,

saw a man, having the exact physical attitudes and wearing the precise clothing and carrying the tan zipper bag that Hereford had described, alight from one of the very trains from the very place stated by Hereford and start to walk at a "fast" pace toward the station exit, Marsh had personally verified every facet of the information given him by Hereford except whether petitioner had accomplished his mission and had the three ounces of heroin on his person or in his bag. And surely, with every other bit of Hereford's information being thus personally verified, Marsh had "reasonable grounds" to believe that the remaining unverified bit of Hereford's information—that Draper would have the heroin with him—was likewise true.

"In dealing with probable cause . . . as the very name implies, we deal with probabilities. These are not technical; they are factual and practical considerations of everyday life on which reasonable and prudent men, not legal technicians, act." . . . Probable cause exists where "the facts and circumstances within their [the arresting officers'] knowledge and of which they had reasonably trustworthy information [are] sufficient in themselves to warrant a man of reasonable caution in the belief that" an offense has been or is being committed. . . .

Justice Douglas, the lone dissenter, did not believe that an informer's tip could equal probable cause unless there was also some personal information on the part of the police.

Draper is an important case for two reasons: it gives us an idea of the factual requirements for probable cause and it introduces us to the problem of informers. Often the police will cite an informer's tip when applying for a search warrant or when justifying a warrantless search after it has occurred. Obviously it is not enough for a policeman to say he conducted (or wants to conduct) a search because an informer told him he'd find evidence of a crime. What *facts* does his informer have to support this conclusion? Do these facts equal probable cause? Why does the policeman believe the informer is reliable?

Probable cause encompasses two things: the information on which the conclusion is based and the reasons for believing the information. When the policeman himself has personal knowledge of the facts alleged to equal probable cause, the defense can cross-examine him if it wishes to prove that in fact no probable cause existed. But when the policeman refers to the tip of an unnamed informer to establish probable cause, the defense may ask that the informer be produced, in order to prove one of the following things: (1) the informer was not, in fact, reliable and the police were not justified in believing the story he told them—the fact that he turned out to be correct cannot, retroactively, establish probable cause; (2) the informer, though reliable in the past, based his information this time on sources which were too speculative to justify a warrant or a warrantless search or arrest; (3) the informer does not exist. The police are lying and have created the informer to justify a search or arrest for which probable cause was entirely lacking.

The state refuses to produce the informer. It argues that it should not be required to produce a reliable informer because public exposure would render him totally useless, if not dead. The informer is an essential ingredient in the solution of crimes and if exposure is required, his effectiveness will cease. The defense, argues the state, can try to prove (1) or (3), of the just-mentioned, by cross-examining the police. Although such cross-examination will not be helpful in proving (2), nevertheless, the state interest in protecting the informer is paramount to the accused's interest in this situation.

In *McCray* v. *Illinois*, 386 U.S. 300 (1967), the Court, five to four, agreed with the state and held that the informer's identity did not have to be revealed. Here are the facts, from Justice Potter Stewart's majority opinion:

The petitioner's arrest occurred near the intersection of 49th Street and Calumet Avenue at about seven in the morning. At the hearing on the motion to suppress, he testified that up until a half hour before he was arrested he had been at "a friend's house" about a block away, that after leaving the friend's house he had "walked with a lady from 48th to 48th and South Park," and that, as he approached 49th Street and Calumet Avenue, "[t]he Officers stopped me going through the alley." "The officers," he said, "did not show me a search warrant for my person or an arrest warrant for my arrest." He said the officers then searched him and found the narcotics in question. The petitioner did not identify the "friend" or the "lady," and neither of them appeared as a witness.

The arresting officers then testified. Officer Jackson stated that he and two fellow officers had had a conversation with an informant on the morning of January 16 in their unmarked police car. The officer said that the informant had told them that the petitioner, with whom Jackson was acquainted, "was selling narcotics and had narcotics on his person and that he could be found in the vicinity of 47th and Calumet at this particular time." Jackson said that he and his fellow officers drove to that vicinity in the police car and that when they spotted the petitioner, the informant pointed him out and then departed on foot. Jackson stated that the officers observed the petitioner walking with a woman, then separating from her and meeting briefly with a man, then proceeding alone, and finally, after seeing the police car, "hurriedly walk[ing] between two buildings." "At this point," Jackson testified, "my partner and myself got out of the car and informed him we had information he had narcotics on his person, placed him in the police vehicle at this point." Jackson stated that the officers then searched the petitioner and found the heroin in a cigarette package.

Jackson testified that he had been acquainted with the informant for approximately a year, that during this period the informant had supplied him with information about narcotics activities "fifteen, sixteen times at least," that the information had proved to be accurate and had resulted in numerous arrests and convictions. On cross-examination, Jackson was even more specific as to the informant's previous reliability, giving the names of people who had been convicted of narcotics violations as the result of information the informant had supplied. When Jackson was asked for the informant's name and address, counsel for the State objected, and the objection was sustained by the court.

Officer Arnold gave substantially the same account of the circumstances of the petitioner's arrest and search, stating that the informant had told the officers that the petitioner "was selling narcotics and had narcotics on his person now in the vicinity of 47th and Calumet." The informant, Arnold testified, "said he had observed [the petitioner] selling narcotics to various people, meaning various addicts, in the area of 47th and Calumet." Arnold testified that he had known the informant "roughly two years," that the informant had given him information concerning narcotics "twenty or twenty-five times," and that the information had resulted in convictions. Arnold too was asked on cross-examination for the informant's name and address, and objections to these questions were sustained by the court.

The Court, after holding that these facts amounted to probable cause and that the informer did not have to be produced, indicated its reliance on the defendant's ability to cross-examine the policemen to protect against the possibility that the "informer rule" would be used to circumvent the probable cause requirement in the Fourth Amendment.

The arresting officers in this case testified, in open court, fully and in precise detail as to what the informer told them and as to why they had reason to believe his information was trustworthy. Each officer was under oath. Each was subjected to searching cross-examination. The judge was obviously satisfied that each was telling the truth, and for that reason he exercised the discretion conferred upon him by the established law of Illinois to respect the informer's privilege.

Nothing in the Due Process Clause of the Fourteenth Amendment requires a state court judge in every such hearing to assume the arresting officers are committing perjury. . . .

The dissent, in an opinion by Justice Douglas, believed (1)

that the police should have secured a warrant by presenting their "tip" to a magistrate, and (2) that the informer should be produced.

There is no way to determine the reliability of Old Reliable, the informer, unless he is produced at the trial and cross-examined. Unless he is produced, the Fourth Amendent is entrusted to the tender mercies of the police. What we do today is to encourage arrests and searches without warrants. The whole momentum of criminal law administration should be in precisely the opposite direction, if the Fourth Amendment is to remain a vital force. Except in rare and emergency cases, it requires magistrates to make the findings of "probable cause." We should be mindful of its command that a judicial mind should be interposed between the police and the citizen. . . .

In the final footnote to his *McCray* dissent, Justice Douglas cited *United States* v. *Pearce,* 275 F.2d 318 (7th Cir. 1960). There, an FBI agent applied for a search warrant "on the basis of confidential information, from a source which in the past has proved reliable." The "information" was received from a superior, whose source was another FBI agent, whose source, in turn, was an informer nobody knew.

Lower court cases after *McCray* recognize that, while it is not always possible to learn the factual basis for the informer's tip, subsequent observations of the suspect's activity often increase the likelihood that the informer is correct. For example, in *Herreres* v. *United States,* 411 F.2d 1198 (9th Cir. 1969), the informer told authorities that a certain car would cross the Mexican border carrying a large amount of heroin. The police observed the car cross the border at the stated time and go to an intersection in a California town. A while later, another driver took the car to Los Angeles where it remained on the street for two days until a third person tried to move it away. The police arrested this third driver and he was convicted of transporting the illegally imported heroin found in the car. On

appeal, his lawyer claimed the informer's identity should have
been revealed so the defendant could show that his conclusion
was not based on probable cause. The appellate court, reject-
ing this argument, held that the suspicious events following the
entrance of the car into the United States sufficiently corroborated the reliability of the informer's conclusion and made his
production unnecessary.

The other area where probable cause presents a problem is
the issuance of warrants. The Fourth Amendment says that
warrants may only issue upon probable cause; what does the
requesting officer actually have to tell the magistrate in order
to get permission to search or arrest?

In *Aguilar* v. *Texas,* a magistrate issued a search warrant on
the basis of the following affidavit:

> Affiants have received reliable information from a credible person
> and do believe that heroin, marijuana, barbiturates, and other
> narcotics and narcotic paraphernalia are being kept at the above
> described premises for the purpose of sale and use contrary to the
> provisions of the law. [378 U.S. 108 (1964)]

This affidavit, in conclusory terms, states both (1) the informer's reliability and (2) the belief that contraband was at
a particular address. The Supreme Court did not believe this
permitted the magistrate to make the independent determination that is his function. Said the Court:

> Although an affidavit may be based on hearsay information and
> need not reflect the direct personal observations of the affiant . . .
> the magistrate must be informed of some of the underlying circum-
> stances from which the informant concluded that the narcotics
> were where he claimed they were, and some of the underlying
> circumstances from which the officer concluded that the informant,
> whose identity need not be disclosed . . . was "credible" or his
> information "reliable." Otherwise, "the inferences from the facts
> which lead to the complaint" will be drawn not "by a neutral and
> detached magistrate," as the Constitution requires, but instead, by

a police officer "engaged in the often competitive enterprise of ferreting out crime," . . . or, as in this case, by an unidentified informant.

Riggan v. *Virginia,* 384 U.S. 152 (1966), involved a numbers game. A police officer secured a warrant to search a particular address where he believed an illegal lottery was being conducted. The basis for his belief, stated in the affidavit to the magistrate was: "Personal observation of the premises and information from sources believed by the police department to be reliable." The Supreme Court summarily reversed the conviction. The Court, citing *Aguilar,* apparently believed the officer's affidavit was defective because it failed to state the facts on which he based his belief that a numbers game was in progress at the particular address. The magistrate, not the officer, had to decide if the officer's facts amounted to probable cause.

Four Justices dissented. They believed the *Riggan* situation differed from *Aguilar.* In *Aguilar,* the officer said that a credible person gave him information that narcotics were kept at a certain address. In *Riggan,* the officer alleged that his belief was based in part on his *own* observations and not an informer's.

But should this difference between the two cases produce a difference in result? In neither case was the magistrate told the facts that the officer relied on for probable cause. If the facts are not stated, how can a magistrate independently determine whether there is probable cause to issue the warrant? And if the magistrate cannot make this determination, why is he there?

In *United States* v. *Ventresca,* 380 U.S. 102 (1965), the Court upheld the issuance of a warrant, though the affidavit submitted by the requesting officer was imperfect. In *Aguilar* and *Riggan,* the officers failed to state the facts from which they inferred probable cause and, therefore, the impartial magistrate could not have made an independent determination. The affidavit in *Ventresca,* however, stated abundant facts to support a finding of probable cause to search. The problem this time was the failure to give the reasons to credit these facts. The requesting officer alleged that his conclusions were based on his own observations and information from other officers. But how did the other officers secure their information? Perhaps an unreliable, private source was involved. Or, perhaps, the other officers also based their information on personal observation. Since the affidavit did not specify the basis for crediting the allegations it contained, how could the magistrate intelligently issue a warrant?

The Court, through Justice Goldberg, acknowledged these defects, but upheld the issuance of the warrant anyway. Its reasons were pragmatic; it said:

[T]he Fourth Amendment's commands, like all constitutional requirements, are practical and not abstract. If the teachings of the Court's cases are to be followed and the constitutional policy served, affidavits for search warrants, such as the one involved here, must be tested and interpreted by magistrates and courts in a common-sense and realistic fashion. They are normally drafted by non-lawyers in the midst and haste of a criminal investigation. Technical requirements of elaborate specificity once exacted under common law pleadings have no proper place in this area. A grudging or negative attitude by reviewing courts towards warrants will tend to discourage police officers from submitting their evidence to a judicial officer before acting.

It was obvious to the Court, just as it was obvious to the magistrate, that the affiant's information was based largely on the personal observations of the investigators assigned to the case. To invalidate the warrant because it failed to spell out the source of the affiant's information in greater detail would be "hypertechnical" and unrealistic. The Chief Justice and Justice Douglas dissented.

Spinelli v. *United States,* 393 U.S. 410 (1969), the last major decision in this area, summarizes much of our discussion of probable cause, informers and warrants. Justice Harlan begins by restating *Aguilar's* "two-pronged test." First, the applicant for a warrant must state the factual circumstances underlying the informant's conclusion. Second, the affidavit must give the reasons to credit the informant or his information. The Court then summarizes the particular affidavit before it.

1. The FBI had kept track of Spinelli's movements on five days during the month of August 1965. On four of these occasions, Spinelli was seen crossing one of two bridges leading from Illinois into St. Louis, Missouri, between 11 A.M. and 12:15 P.M. On four of the five days, Spinelli was also seen parking his car in a lot used by residents of an apartment house at 1108 Indian Circle Drive in St. Louis, between 3:30 P.M. and 4:45 P.M. On one day, Spinelli was followed further and seen to enter a particular apartment in the building.

2. An FBI check with the telephone company revealed that this apartment contained two telephones listed under the name of Grace P. Hagen, and carrying the numbers WYdown 4–0029 and WYdown 4–0136.

3. The application stated that "William Spinelli is known to this affiant and to federal law enforcement agents and local law enforcement agents as a bookmaker, an associate of bookmakers, a gambler, and an associate of gamblers."

4. Finally, it was stated that the FBI "has been informed by a confidential reliable informant that William Spinelli is operating a handbook and accepting wagers and disseminating wagering information by means of the telephones which have been assigned the numbers WYdown 4–0029 and WYdown 4–0136."

The Court held that paragraphs 1 and 2 were insufficient to establish probable cause. Paragraph 3, said the Court, "is but a bald and unilluminating assertion of suspicion that is entitled to no weight in appraising the magistrate's decision." All depended on paragraph 4—the informer's tip. The Government argued that the tip lent a suspicious color to the apparently innocent activity in paragraphs 1 and 2, and that, conversely, "the FBI's surveillance corroborates the informant's tip, thereby entitling it to more weight."

The Court rejected this argument. It noted that there are two ways in which a magistrate may properly decide to credit an informant's tip. First, in line with *Aguilar*, the basis for the informant's conclusion and the reasons for believing the informant might be stated in the affidavit. This was not done in the conclusory language of paragraph 4. Second, the independent observations of the police might corroborate the informant's tip in sufficient detail to establish probable cause. Recall *Draper* and *Herreres*.

Applying this second test, the *Spinelli* affidavit failed again. The facts in paragraphs 1 and 2 did not supply sufficient corroboration of the tip "to support both the inference that the informer was generally trustworthy and that he had made his charge against Spinelli on the basis of information obtained in a reliable way."

A complete reading of the majority opinion in *Spinelli* will show how carefully the Court dissects the affidavit in issue. The Court demands real, not automatic, inspection from the issuing magistrate. Is this perhaps a reaction to *McCray*? *McCray* weakened the protection given the defendant at one stage of the process; does *Spinelli* try to compensate by strengthening the protection at an earlier stage?

IV   Stop and Frisk

Here is a variation on a "probable cause" problem that has intrigued law students for years. A policeman is walking through the lobby of a luxurious hotel. He sees a man, dressed in very shabby clothing, emerge from a room where a large party is in progress. The man is carrying an expensive fur coat. His walk is casual and there is nothing suspicious about his demeanor. The officer knows that the party was billed as a costume ball. The man is heading toward the street. Is there probable cause for arrest?

Consider another example. A policeman turns a corner and

finds a woman who has just been mugged. She tells him a man, about six-feet tall, knocked her down and took her purse. A few minutes later, the policeman sees a man walking quickly down a side street, one arm pressed to his side as though he were holding something against his body beneath his coat. When he sees the policeman, he walks faster. But the man is only five-feet tall. The policeman knows that mugging victims do not always give correct descriptions of their attackers. Is there probable cause for arrest?

At about the same time each day, a policeman observes that a man goes into a barber shop, takes something out of his pocket, receives money from the barber, and leaves. This continues for ten days. The barber shop was once headquarters for the neighborhood's numbers racket, but that supposedly stopped when its previous owner was arrested a year ago. The man under observation has two convictions for "numbers" violations. In each case he was a runner. But these convictions are eight years old. The suspect has no visible means of support. Is there probable cause for arrest?

In each of these crimes, there is more than just suspicion that a crime is being committed by the suspect. The question is whether there is enough to justify an arrest? If probable cause is always needed for arrest, the answer will depend on what is meant by probable cause. The more strictly the term is defined, the more the police will have to show. If probable cause is broadly defined, many more people will be subject to arrest though the likelihood of guilt is smaller. Arrest is at best a great annoyance, and at worst it can severely and irreparably affect the arrested person's life. Therefore, it is preferable to permit arrest only in those situations where the likelihood of guilt is greater than in our three examples.

On the other hand, if the officer in each of our three cases merely stopped the person under observation and asked for an explanation of his activity, the violation of the suspect's liberty is substantially less and the officer may be able to satisfy himself that a crime is not being committed. Even though there is no probable cause for search or arrest, there might be sufficient reason simply to stop and question. Is there such a thing as stopping, apart from arresting? Can a police officer search after a stop, as he can after an arrest?[4] If, after stopping, the suspect does not give an adequate explanation of his activities, is there then probable cause to arrest?

In *Terry* v. *Ohio,* 392 U.S. 1 (1968), the Court dealt with this problem for the first time. Chief Justice Earl Warren's opinion was a new attempt to balance the interests of society in investigating suspicious behavior and the interests of the individual members of society in freedom from police restraint. Until *Terry,* these interests were balanced by invocation of the phrase "probable cause." If probable cause was present, the invasion was permissible. If there was no probable cause, the individual interest prevailed. *Terry* was an attempt to deal with gradations of invasions by applying a less strict standard than probable cause. If the individual suffers something less than an arrest or search (as we have been using these words), should society be permitted to investigate on something less than probable cause?[5]

The facts in *Terry,* as in most of the cases in this area, are important. While Officer McFadden

was patrolling in plain clothes in downtown Cleveland at approximately 2:30 in the afternoon of October 31, 1963, his attention was attracted by two men, Chilton and Terry, standing on the corner of Huron Road and Euclid Avenue. He had never seen the two men before, and he was unable to say precisely what first drew his eye to them. However, he testified that he had been a policeman for thirty-nine years and a detective for thirty-five and that he had been assigned to patrol this vicinity of downtown Cleveland for

---

[4] Recall that one of the underlying reasons for permitting a search incident to an arrest is to protect the arresting officer. Isn't that reason similarly present where only a stop is involved?

[5] See also two companion cases to *Terry: Peters* v. *New York, Sibron* v. *New York,* 392 U.S. 41 (1968).

shoplifters and pickpockets for thirty years. He explained that he had developed routine habits of observation over the years and that he would "stand and watch people or walk and watch people at many intervals of the day." He added: "Now, in this case when I looked over they didn't look right to me at the time."

His interest aroused, Officer McFadden took up a post of observation in the entrance to a store 300 to 400 feet away from the two men. "I get more purpose to watch them when I seen their movements," he testified. He saw one of the men leave the other one and walk southwest on Huron Road, past some stores. The man paused for a moment and looked in a store window, then walked on a short distance, turned around and walked back toward the corner, pausing once again to look in the same store window. He rejoined his companion at the corner, and the two conferred briefly. Then the second man went through the same series of motions, strolling down Huron Road, looking in the same window, walking on a short distance, turning back, peering in the store window again, and returning to confer with the first man at the corner. The two men repeated this ritual alternately between five and six times a piece—in all, roughly a dozen trips. At one point, while the two were standing together on the corner, a third man approached them and engaged them briefly in conversation. This man then left the two others and walked west on Euclid Avenue. Chilton and Terry resumed their measured pacing, peering, and conferring. After this had gone on for ten to twelve minutes, the two men walked off together heading west on Euclid Avenue, following the path taken earlier by the third man.

By this time Officer McFadden had become thoroughly suspicious. He testified that after observing their elaborately casual and oft-repeated reconnaissance of the store window on Huron Road, he suspected the two men of "casing a job, a stick-up," and that he considered it his duty as a police officer to investigate further. He added that he feared "they may have a gun." Thus, Officer McFadden followed Chilton and Terry and saw them stop in front of Zucker's store to talk to the same man who had conferred with them earlier on the street corner. Deciding that the situation was ripe for direct action, Officer McFadden approached the three men, identified himself as a police officer and asked for their names. At this point his knowledge was confined to what he had observed. He was not acquainted with any of the three men by name or by sight, and he had received no information concerning them from any other source. When the men "mumbled something" in response to his inquiries, Officer McFadden grabbed petitioner Terry, spun him around so that they were facing the other two, with Terry between McFadden and the others, and patted down the outside of his clothing. In the left breast pocket of Terry's overcoat Officer McFadden felt a pistol. He reached inside the overcoat pocket, but was unable to remove the gun. At this point, keeping Terry between himself and the others, the officer ordered all three men to enter Zucker's store. As they went in, he removed Terry's overcoat completely, retrieved a .38-caliber revolver from the pocket and ordered all three men to face the wall with their hands raised. Officer McFadden proceeded to pat down the outer clothing of Chilton and the third man, Katz. He discovered another revolver in the outer pocket of Chilton's overcoat, but no weapons were found on Katz. The officer testified that he only patted the men down to see whether they had weapons, and that he did not put his hands beneath the outer garments of either Terry or Chilton until he felt their guns. So far as appears from the record, he never placed his hands beneath Katz's outer garments. Officer McFadden seized Chilton's gun, asked the proprietor of the store to call a police wagon, and took all three men to the station, where Chilton and Terry were formally charged with carrying concealed weapons. . . .

The Court acknowledged that these facts thrust "to the fore difficult and troublesome issues regarding a sensitive area of police activity." Some argued that "the police are in need of an escalating set of flexible responses, graduated in relation to the amount of information they possess." Others argued "that the authority of the police must be strictly circumscribed by the law of arrest and search as it has developed to date in the traditional jurisprudence of the Fourth Amendment."

The Court approached the facts before it against this background and in light of the following considerations on the effectiveness of the exclusionary rule in stop and frisk situations.

The exclusionary rule has its limitations . . . as a tool of judicial control. . . . [Street] encounters are initiated by the police for a wide variety of purposes, some of which are wholly unrelated to a desire to prosecute for crime. Doubtless some police "field interrogation" conduct violates the Fourth Amendment. But a stern refusal by this Court to condone such activity does not necessarily render it responsive to the exclusionary rule. Regardless of how effective the rule may be where obtaining convictions is an important objective of the police, it is powerless to deter invasions of constitutionally guaranteed rights where the police either have no interest in prosecuting or are willing to forego successful prosecution in the interest of serving some other goal.

The Court declined to use the words "stop" and "frisk"; rather, it indicated that these were degrees of "search" and "seizure." The extent of the official invasion must be balanced against the quality and quantity of information possessed. The greater the intrusion, the more information is required. But what is the balance? Until now it has always been probable cause. If it existed, the officer could arrest or search. Otherwise, he could not. What is the new balance and when does it apply?

To answer this question, it is first necessary to recall the odd wording of the Fourth Amendment:

The right of the people to be secure . . . against unreasonable searches and seizures, shall not be violated, and no Warrants shall issue, but upon probable cause. . . .

The Amendment is divided into two independent clauses. The standard for searches and seizures is reasonableness, but the standard for a warrant is probable cause. The Amendment says nothing about when a warrant must be secured, thus triggering the stricter probable cause standard.

The Court held that the facts before it did not require the warrant procedure because of exigent circumstances—if Mc-Fadden had gone off for a warrant, he could not have been around for the ensuing action. Therefore, "the conduct involved in this case must be tested by the Fourth Amendment's general proscription against unreasonable searches and seizures." Reasonableness was the test.

Thus the Court, in a few dozen words, gave a whole new perspective to the law of search and seizure. The potential for the *Terry* rationale is huge. Every search and arrest that can be made under an exception to the warrant requirement need only be reasonable and it need not necessarily be based on probable cause. Take the automobile exception, as an example. The reason it is an exception at all is that automobiles are mobile and there is no time to present the facts to a magistrate. But does this reason for dropping the magistrate also justify dropping probable cause as the standard? No; under these facts, other things being equal, reasonableness should be taken to mean probable cause.

Even when the standard is reasonableness, the law requires more than a hunch; it requires "specific and articulable facts" which can eventually "be subjected to the more detached, neutral scrutiny of a judge who must evaluate the reasonableness of a particular search or seizure in light of the particular circumstances." On the specific facts before it, the Court held McFadden's investigation proper.

But what about the ensuing search, which actually turned up the gun? Was that proper, and what was its permissible scope? The Court said:

[S]uch a search, unlike a search without a warrant incident to a lawful arrest, is not justified by any need to prevent the disappearance or destruction of evidence of crime. . . . The sole justification of the search in the present situation is the protection of the police officer and others nearby, and it must therefore be confined in scope to an intrusion reasonably designed to discover guns, knives, clubs, or other hidden instruments for the assault of the police officer.

The scope of the search in this case presents no serious problem in light of these standards. Officer McFadden patted down the outer clothing of petitioner and his two companions. He did not place his hands in their pockets or under the outer surface of their garments until he had felt weapons, and then he merely reached for and removed the guns. He never did invade Katz's person beyond the outer surfaces of his clothes, since he discovered nothing in his pat down which might have been a weapon. Officer McFadden confined his search strictly to what was minimally necessary to learn whether the men were armed and to disarm them once he discovered the weapons. He did not conduct a general exploratory search for whatever evidence of criminal activity he might find. . . .

Justice Douglas was the sole dissenter.

In *Terry,* the policeman's actions were not specifically authorized by a statute. In some states there are statutes expressing a legislative determination of the degree of police interference that will be tolerated on the basis of a standard of less than probable cause. These legislative determinations will be acceptable to the Supreme Court and indeed, welcomed, so long as they do not authorize action condemned by the Constitution. In New York, the new Criminal Procedure Law[6] states:

1. In addition to the authority provided by this article for making an arrest without a warrant, a police officer may stop a person in a public place located within the geographical area of such officer's employment when he reasonably suspects that such person is committing, has committed or is about to commit either (a) a felony or (b) a class A misdemeanor defined in the penal law, and may demand of him his name, address and an explanation of his conduct.

2. When upon stopping a person under circumstances prescribed in subdivision one a police officer reasonably suspects that he is in danger of physical injury, he may search such person for a deadly weapon or any instrument, article or substance readily capable of causing serious physical injury and of a sort not ordinarily carried in public places by law-abiding persons. If he finds such a weapon or instrument, or any other property possession of which he reasonably believes may constitute the commission of a crime, he may take it and keep it until the completion of the questioning, at which time he shall either return it, if lawfully possessed, or arrest such person.

Perhaps *Terry*-type intrusions will lead to fewer abuses of power, if, as with the New York statute, they are permitted only

[6] Effective Sept. 1, 1971.

when an officer reasonably suspects a felony or a serious misdemeanor.

In *Davis* v. *Mississippi,* 394 U.S. 721 (1969), an interesting post-*Terry* decision, the Court hinted that some standard of less than probable cause might permit detention for a brief period in order to take a suspect's fingerprints. The Court noted that fingerprinting "involves none of the probing into an individual's private life and thoughts which marks an interrogation or search." Since police need only one set of prints, there is no danger of harassment by repeated detention. The Court noted, however, that because there is no danger that fingerprints might be destroyed, the prior authorization of a judicial officer may be required before an individual can be detained for the purpose of taking his fingerprints. *Davis* is an indication of the Court's willingness to employ standards less strict than probable cause when the state invasion is less than a traditional arrest or search.[7]

---

[7] Recently, the Burger Court, relatively inactive in the criminal law area, created an additional exception to traditional Fourth Amendment requirements. In his first majority opinion, Justice Harry Blackmun upheld the constitutionality of a statute permitting a caseworker to enter a welfare resident's home against her will and even though he had no reason to believe a crime was being or had been committed. *Wyman* v. *James,* decided Jan. 12, 1971.

5

WIRETAPPING AND EAVESDROPPING:

OLD RULES

AND NEW TECHNIQUES

The law of wiretapping and electronic eavesdropping winds its way through the twentieth century's major judicial opinions. It begins in 1928 with the famous case of *Olmstead* v. *United States* and ends, for the moment, thirty-nine years later with the equally noteworthy case of *Katz* v. *United States.*

The issue is and has usually been: what does the Fourth Amendment, and therefore, the Fourteenth, demand when the government taps a wire or overhears a conversation with an electronic device? Are these actions subject to constitutional control? If so, does the Constitution forbid all eavesdropping and wiretapping? If we must balance the value of individual privacy against the need to solve crime, where does the balance lie?

Once these "policy" questions are answered, we must reconcile the answers with the particular language in the Constitution. For example, can a conversation be "searched" or "seized?" Can it be "particularly described?" The people have the right to be secure in their "persons, houses, papers, and effects." Do any of these designations encompass conversations?

Wiretapping, Eavesdropping, and Undercover Agents

Wiretapping refers to the interception of the content of a telephonic or telegraphic communication by one who is not a party to that communication. This is generally done by attaching a listening device to the transmission wires. However, listening in on an extension phone without permission is also wiretapping.

Wiretapping may be accomplished without entering the home or office of the suspect. In other words, the only transgression may be to the wire itself. On the other hand, entrance into a protected area to place the tap is also possible. In such a case, the legality of the entrance and the legality of the tap are both in question.

These alternative possibilities also apply to "electronic eavesdropping," which refers to the act of overhearing a conversation with the aid of a mechanical device, often electronic. Overhearing a conversation on a park bench or in a bus is not included, nor is pressing the unaided ear to the wall. The law is concerned with the use of devices to overhear conversations which the participants reasonably expect are private. (Compare the protection against unreasonable searches when a protected area, like a home, is involved and when an unprotected area, like an open field, is the issue.)

This chapter is limited to invasions of conversational privacy. For example, there are cameras that can take pictures in total darkness, with the aid of infrared light. There are telescopes that can focus through windows from blocks away. Cameras in the telescope's lens can photograph the image at the other end. There are additional ways to invade privacy with aids to the eye rather than the ear. The law has barely developed in this area and we can only speculate on the outcome. For instance, do the safeguards against invasions of conversational privacy apply with equal strength to telescopic invasions that permit the observer to read the lips of the observed?[1]

There is a third method of privacy invasion, somewhat like electronic eavesdropping and wiretapping, except that it does not necessarily involve the use of mechanical devices. This method uses an undercover agent, someone who gains entrance to a protected area, or is able to overhear or engage in conversations with a suspect, by pretending to be someone else. In this situation, the suspect is aware of the agent's presence but he is unaware of his purpose. A suspect may believe he is talking to a co-conspirator, while his listener is really a law officer.

Undercover agents in these situations may equip themselves with electronic recording or broadcasting devices. The broadcasting device permits another agent, in a different place, to overhear and record what is said. An undercover agent may carry a listening device, if feasible, to help assure conviction at trial. For example, if an Internal Revenue agent claims John Q. Taxpayer attempted to bribe him, and Mr. Taxpayer testifies that the agent makes his accusation only because the taxpayer did not respond to a bribe solicitation, the jury will have to decide who is lying. If the agent recorded the entire conversation, conviction is likely.

The law in these three areas of privacy invasion—electronic eavesdropping, wiretapping, and undercover agents—has developed significantly during the second half of the 1960s. Therefore, we shall consider the rules prior to 1966 and then the more recent developments.

The Law to 1966

The case that first considered this subject in detail is partially responsible for the confusion during the next forty years. In *Olmstead* v. *United States,* 277 U.S. 438 (1928), a bare ma-

---

[1] For an account of the various privacy-invading gadgets, see Alan F. Westin, *Privacy and Freedom,* Ch. 4 (New York: Atheneum, 1967).

jority, in an opinion by Chief Justice William H. Taft, simply held that a message, traveling along a telephone wire, was not protected by the Fourth Amendment. Therefore, interception had no constitutional sanction and the overheard conversation and its fruits could be admitted in court.

Chief Justice Taft read the literal language of the Fourth Amendment and determined that it did not apply to telephonic messages. "The Amendment itself shows that the search is to be of material things—the person, the house, his papers or his effects. The description of the warrant necessary to make the proceeding lawful, is that it must specify the place to be searched and the person or *things* to be seized." Conversations were not "things."

In his dissent, Justice Holmes saw the need to make a basic policy determination. He said: "We have to choose, and for my part I think it is a less evil that some criminals should escape than that the Government should play an ignoble part."

Justice Louis Brandeis wrote a long, often-quoted dissent. He reminded the Court that it had

repeatedly sustained the exercise of power by Congress, under various clauses of [the Constitution], over objects of which the Fathers could not have dreamed. . . . We have likewise held that general limitations on the powers of Government, like those embodied in the Due Process Clauses of the Fifth and Fourteenth Amendments, do not forbid the United States or the States from meeting modern conditions by regulations which "a century ago, or even half a century ago, probably would have been rejected as arbitrary and oppressive." Clauses guaranteeing to the individual protection against specific abuses of power, must have a similar capacity of adaptation to a changing world.

Justice Brandeis continued:

When the Fourth and Fifth Amendments were adopted, "the form that evil had theretofore taken," had been necessarily simple. Force and violence were then the only means known to man by which a Government could directly effect self-incrimination. It could compel the individual to testify—a compulsion effected, if need be, by torture. It could secure possession of his papers and other articles incident to his private life—a seizure effected, if need be, by breaking and entry. Protections against such invasion of "the sanctities of a man's home and the privacies of life" was provided in the Fourth and Fifth Amendments by specific language. . . . But "time works changes, brings into existence new conditions and purposes." Subtler and more far-reaching means of invading privacy have become available to the Government. Discovery and invention have made it possible for the Government, by means far more effective than stretching upon the rack, to obtain disclosure in court of what is whispered in the closet.

Moreover, "in the application of a constitution, our contemplation cannot be only of what has been but of what may be." The progress of science in furnishing the Government with means of espionage is not likely to stop with wire-tapping. Ways may some day be developed by which the Government, without removing papers from secret drawers, can reproduce them in court, and by which it will be enabled to expose to a jury the most intimate occurrences of the home. Advances in the psychic and related sciences may bring means of exploring unexpressed beliefs, thoughts and emotions.

The *Olmstead* majority did not have the foresight of the dissent with the consequence that for forty years only "material things," and not conversations, received Fourth Amendment protection. Legislative protection was still possible after *Olmstead,* however, and six years later, in Section 605 of the Federal Communications Act of 1934, Congress said:

[N]o person not being authorized by the sender shall intercept any communication and divulge or publish the existence, contents, substance, purport, effect, or meaning of such intercepted communications to any person. . . .

Section 605 is still law today.[2] The Supreme Court has in-

[2] It has been amended to conform with the 1968 Crime Control and Safe Streets Act, described below.

terpreted it to apply to all persons, including federal and state law enforcement personnel.

But two early developments diluted the strength of Section 605. The FBI and the Justice Department decided that the law did not prohibit wiretapping, but only wiretapping that is followed by divulgence to any person who is not another member of the government. Consequently, law enforcement officers believed they could continue tapping wires. A second limitation on Section 605 was that state courts generally admitted evidence that was the product of a wiretap even though to do so constituted "divulgence" under Section 605 and, therefore, a violation of federal law. For a long time, the Supreme Court refused to enjoin this state court action. *Schwartz* v. *Texas,* 344 U.S. 199 (1952).[3]

Section 605 is not applicable when the interception is accomplished with the consent of one of the parties to the conversation. *Rathbun* v. *United States,* 355 U.S. 107 (1957). "Each party to a telephone conversation takes the risk that the other party may have an extension telephone and may allow another to overhear the conversation." This rule is still the law and, although the case involved an extension phone, the rule probably applies to all consensual tapping.

Electronic eavesdropping raised similar problems prior to 1966 and was, similarly, blanketly excluded from constitutional control. Justice Brandeis's prophetic dissent was becoming true. Technology was developing amazing gadgets that could be used in the business of privacy invasion. Parabolic microphones could pick up conversations hundreds of feet away. Telephones could be transformed to constant listening devices, even with the receiver on the hook. A miniature microphone could be substituted for the button of a suit jacket, wire substituted for thread, turning the wearer into a walking transmitter.

---

[3] However, in *Lee* v. *Florida,* 392 U.S. 378 (1968), the Court held that state courts could no longer admit evidence secured in violation of a federal statute.

Yet in 1942, the Supreme Court said law enforcement officers could electronically eavesdrop so long as they did not otherwise violate the privacy of the suspect. In other words, the mere use of an eavesdropping device was not a violation. In *Goldman* v. *United States,* 316 U.S. 129 (1942), federal officers overheard certain conversations by pressing a detectaphone against the outside wall of the defendant's private office. The Court said there was no Fourth Amendment violation because there was no actual invasion of the office itself. Compare *Silverman* v. *United States,* 365 U.S. 505 (1961), where federal officers inserted a spike mike into a party wall of defendants' house. The mike made contact with a heating duct, "thus converting their entire heating system into a conductor of sound." A unanimous Court held these events constituted a violation of the defendants' Fourth Amendment rights. In *Silverman* the officers made the technical mistake of letting the mike touch part of the defendants' residence and not, as in *Goldman,* only the outside wall. Justice Douglas thought these trivial differences should not cause a difference in result. "Our sole concern," he said, "should be with whether the privacy of the home was invaded." The answer to this question should not turn on "nice distinctions."

Undercover agents also escaped Fourth Amendment control prior to 1966. The two major cases are *On Lee* v. *United States,* 343 U.S. 747 (1952), and *Lopez* v. *United States,* 373 U.S. 427 (1963).

In *On Lee,* the defendant had been arrested and released on bail, and he was awaiting indictment, when an acquaintance, Chin Poy, engaged him in conversation. The government had equipped Chin Poy with a hidden microphone, enabling an agent to overhear the conversation. At On Lee's trial, the agent testified to what he had heard and the Supreme Court upheld the admissibility of this testimony.

In *Lopez,* an Internal Revenue agent pretended to go along with a taxpayer's attempted bribe while recording his conversations with the taxpayer on a hidden wire recorder. The Supreme Court held the recordings properly admitted at the trial. Justice Harlan wrote:

Stripped to its essentials, petitioner's argument amounts to saying that he has a constitutional right to rely on possible flaws in the agent's memory, or to challenge the agent's credibility without being beset by corroborating evidence that is not susceptible of impeachment. For no other argument can justify excluding an accurate version of a conversation that the agent could testify to from memory. We think the risk that petitioner took in offering a bribe to Davis fairly included the risk that the offer would be accurately reproduced in court, whether by faultless memory or mechanical recording.

Justice Brennan, joined by Justices Douglas and Goldberg, agreed that Lopez took the risk that the agent would divulge the conversation, but believed he did not take

the risk that third parties, whether mechanical auditors like the Minifon or human transcribers of mechanical transmissions as in *On Lee*—third parties who cannot be shut out of a conversation as conventional eavesdroppers can be, merely by a lowering of voices, or withdrawing to a private place—may give independent evidence of any conversation. There is only one way to guard against such a risk, and that is to keep one's mouth shut on all occasions.

Undercover agents, with or without mechanical devices, are essential to police work. Prior to 1966, the Supreme Court was unwilling to place substantial Fourth Amendment restrictions on their use. A minority of justices, however, believed that the Constitution prevented the uncontrolled use of mechanical devices and that such uncontrolled use would eventually stifle even legitimate conversation.

The Law After 1966

UNDERCOVER AGENTS

Three cases decided by the Supreme Court on December 12, 1966, confirmed the rule that a person takes the risk that the recipient of his confidence might betray him. The Fourth Amendment does not protect him. However, one of the three cases involved an undercover agent equipped with a recording device, and there the Court intimated that the Fourth Amendment did apply.

In 1962, James Hoffa was on trial in Nashville, Tennessee for violation of the Taft-Hartley Act. A minor Teamsters Union official, Edward Partin, made repeated visits to Hoffa's hotel room during the course of the trial and reported to the FBI conversations between Hoffa and others about attempts to bribe jurors.[4] Eventually, Hoffa was tried for jury tampering, and Partin's testimony contributed to his conviction. On appeal to the Supreme Court, Hoffa claimed that the government's use of Partin violated his Fourth, Fifth, and Sixth Amendment rights. The Court, assuming Partin was a government agent who went to Hoffa's hotel room initially in that capacity,[5] nevertheless affirmed the convictions. *Hoffa* v. *United States,* 385 U.S. 293 (1966).

The Court rejected Hoffa's argument that by using an informer to gain its information the government violated the Fourth Amendment. Although a hotel room is a protected area, the Court reasoned that Hoffa "was not relying on the security of the hotel room; he was relying on his misplaced confidence

[4] Partin was paid by the government both in money and with his freedom: at the time, he was under a federal indictment, and several state charges were pending.

[5] The government had claimed that Partin visited Hoffa's room originally to discuss union business, but had cooperated with the FBI only after learning of the jury tampering.

that Partin would not reveal his wrongdoing." The Court continued:

Neither this Court nor any member of it has ever expressed the view that the Fourth Amendment protects a wrongdoer's misplaced belief that a person to whom he voluntarily confides his wrongdoing will not reveal it. Indeed, the Court unanimously rejected that very contention less than four years ago in Lopez v. United States. . . .[6]

The facts in *Osborn* v. *United States,* 385 U.S. 323 (1966), were like those in *Lopez,* except that *Osborn* involved an attorney who attempted to bribe a juror instead of a taxpayer's bribe of an IRS agent. Like his counterpart in *Lopez,* the undercover agent in *Osborn* carried a concealed recorder and the Supreme Court was eventually asked to rule on the constitutional propriety of this tactic.

Osborn's conviction was affirmed. The noteworthy point about the case is the apparent retreat by the Court from the broad holding in *Lopez* that the Fourth Amendment is not concerned with recorder-carrying informers. In *Osborn,* the undercover agent was authorized by two federal judges to carry the concealed recorder after he reported on attempts to bribe jurors. The Supreme Court, holding that it did not have to "rest our decision here upon the broad foundation of the Court's opinion in *Lopez* . . . ," continued:

The issue here, therefore, is not the permissibility of "indiscriminate use of such devices in law enforcement," but the permissibility of using such a device under the most precise and discriminate circumstances, circumstances which fully meet the "requirement of particularity" which the dissenting opinion in *Lopez* found necessary. . . .

[I]n response to a detailed factual affidavit alleging the com-

---

[6] The Court also rejected Hoffa's Fifth and Sixth Amendment arguments, but that portion of the opinion does not concern us. Justice Douglas and Justice Clark did not believe the Court should have reviewed the conviction at all. Chief Justice Warren dissented on the merits.

mission of a specific criminal offense directly and immediately affecting the administration of justice in the federal court, the judges of that court jointly authorized the use of a recording device for the narrow and particularized purpose of ascertaining the truth of the affidavit's allegations. . . . There could hardly be a clearer example of "the procedure of antecedent justification before a magistrate that is central to the Fourth Amendment" as "a precondition of lawful electronic surveillance."

Justice Brennan, who had dissented in *Lopez,* concurred in *Osborn.* Justice Douglas dissented in both *Lopez* and *Osborn.*

In *Lewis* v. *United States,* 385 U.S. 206 (1966), the final case in the trilogy, the simple question was "whether the Fourth Amendment was violated when a federal narcotics agent, by misrepresenting his identity and stating his willingness to purchase narcotics, was invited into petitioner's home where an unlawful narcotics transaction was consummated and the narcotics were thereafter introduced at petitioner's criminal trial." Since the agent entered the petitioner's home "for the specific purpose of executing a felonious sale of narcotics," and since he did not "see, hear, or take anything that was not contemplated, and in fact intended, by petitioner as a necessary part of his illegal business," the Fourth Amendment would not protect the petitioner, who took the risk and therefore could not complain.

The rules respecting undercover agents did not change significantly after 1966. The actor takes the chance that his confidant will betray him. However, when the agent carries electronic recording or transmitting devices, there is an indication that *Lopez* and *On Lee* may have been limited by *Osborn. Osborn* seemed to say that electronic devices may not be used indiscriminately by undercover agents and that some prior authorization or at least justification for their use is required.

Should the police be free to use undercover agents, even without recording devices, indiscriminately? The Court seems to believe there is a difference between agents and listening devices

because a suspect knows the agent is there and takes the risk
that he will inform, while a listening device is necessarily hidden.
But if risk-taking is the criterion, the Court could consistently
hold that a suspect also takes the risk that a hidden device will
overhear him. Perhaps the real reason listening devices receive
Fourth Amendment protection is that we want the police to
have probable cause before such devices are randomly used.
If they are used on suspicion, too many innocent people would
be subject to a form of privacy invasion we reject. When probable cause is established, we do, in fact, force the speaker to
take the risk, but we accept this invasion because the existence
of probable cause has tipped the scale in favor of the state.

The same reasoning can be applied to undercover agents.
It would be as shocking to discover a transmitter in our living
room as to learn that one of our best friends was ordered to
work his way into our life and report all we did. Before an
agent is used, there should also be probable cause to believe
he'll find something. In *Lewis,* the agent called seeking to buy
narcotics, and Lewis's agreement to sell created probable cause
to continue the subterfuge. Furthermore, the agent did not pick
Lewis's name out of the phone book but had information that
Lewis was a dealer. Consequently, the Supreme Court wasn't
faced with the problem of an indiscriminate use of an undercover agent. But the use of such agents for "fishing expedi-
tions" must not automatically be excluded from constitutional
protection simply because mechanical devices are not involved.[7]

Since the circumstances under which an undercover informer may be used are diverse, the facts that will supply
probable cause will vary. For example, if the police believe
narcotics are being sold in a particular neighborhood, that

[7] A lawyer who has represented both the prosecution and the defense
in criminal trials tells me that in both roles, he prefers to have undercover informers carry recording devices. The recording supports the
prosecution case by corroborating the informer's testimony. On the other
hand, the recording also serves as a check on the informer's memory or
imagination.

should be sufficient cause to have an agent attempt to make a purchase in that neighborhood. On the other hand, something more than suspicion should be required before an undercover agent is allowed to spend months winning an individual's confidence.

Finally, an individual will not be guilty of a crime if his actions result from the creative energies of an undercover agent. This is called entrapment, and it is a valid defense whenever an alleged crime would not have occurred but for the inducement of the undercover agent. A classic example of entrapment is when an agent plays upon the sympathies of a suspect and begs him to get the agent a fix before "withdrawal" gets worse. The suspect who succumbs in that situation is not guilty. *Sherman* v. *United States,* 356 U.S. 369 (1958).

WIRETAPPING AND EAVESDROPPING

The Court's scrutiny of the circumstances surrounding the use of the recorder-carrying agent in *Osborn* suggested the imminent end of the *Olmstead* era. Some thought the end came in *Berger* v. *New York,* 388 U.S. 41 (1967), but we now know this is not true (*Kaiser* v. *New York,* 394 U.S. 280 [1969]). The *coup de grâce* was administered a few months later in *Katz* v. *United States,* 389 U.S. 347 (1967).

In *Berger,* under the authority of a New York statute, police placed eavesdropping devices in the office of Mr. Harry Steinman. After listening for two weeks, they uncovered a conspiracy in the issuance of liquor licenses, and Berger was convicted on the basis of evidence secured from the eavesdrop. Since the police entered Steinman's office to place the bug, the case could be resolved with a finding that this trespass violated the Fourth Amendment. It was unnecessary to reconsider *Olmstead* and decide whether the eavesdrop alone would have been constitutional.

The State claimed that the office trespass met Fourth Amendment requirements since the police, acting under a state law, had obtained a valid warrant to enter Steinman's office and place the bug. So far so good. But the Fourth Amendment has additional requirements—for example, that the object of the search (here, conversations) be particularly described. Thus, *Berger* raised the very interesting question of whether the New York statute, authorizing a physical trespass on a protected area to seize conversations, was constitutional. We know the police can secure a warrant on probable cause to search for and seize money or heroin. But the law in *Berger* permitted a trespass to plant a microphone. Could this be done?

Berger's partial answer to this question is particularly important now that *Katz* has held conversations themselves protected by the Fourth Amendment. *Berger's* treatment of a statute authorizing a trespass to seize conversations is now equally applicable to seizures of conversations accomplished without a trespass. What must a statute authorizing the seizure of a conversation contain? Is the federal law discussed at the end of this Chapter constitutional?

The New York law in *Berger* authorized certain judicial officers to grant orders for eavesdropping upon "oath or affirmation of a district attorney, or of the attorney general or of an officer above the rank of sergeant of any police department." The oath had to state "that there is reasonable ground to believe that evidence of a crime may" be obtained. It also had to name the particular persons whose conversations would be overheard. The issuing judge had to be satisfied, after examining the applicant, that there was reasonable ground to grant the request. The order had to specify its duration, but it could not last more than two months, unless extended. Five Justices said this statute was unconstitutional, and a sixth concurred in the result, for the following reasons:

First, as we have mentioned, eavesdropping is authorized without requiring belief that any particular offense has been or is being committed; nor that the property sought, the conversations, be particularly described. The purpose of the probable cause requirement of the Fourth Amendment to keep the state out of constitutionally protected areas until it has reason to believe that a specific crime has been or is being committed is thereby wholly aborted. Likewise, the statute's failure to describe with particularity the conversations sought gives the officer a roving commission to seize any and all conversations. It is true that the statute requires the naming of "the person or persons whose communications, conversations or discussions are to be overheard or recorded. . . ." But this does no more than identify the person whose constitutionally protected area is to be invaded rather than "particularly describing" the communications, conversations, or discussions to be seized. As with general warrants this leaves too much to the discretion of the officer executing the order. Secondly, authorization of eavesdropping for a two-month period is the equivalent of a series of intrusions, searches, and seizures pursuant to a single showing of probable cause. Prompt execution is also avoided. During such a long and continuous (twenty-four hours a day) period the conversations of any and all persons coming into the area covered by the device will be seized indiscriminately and without regard to their connection to the crime under investigation. Moreover, the statute permits, as was done here, extensions of the original two-month period—presumably for two months each—on a mere showing that such extension is "in the public interest." Apparently the original grounds on which the eavesdrop order was initially issued also form the basis of the renewal. This we believe insufficient without a showing of present probable cause for the continuance of the eavesdrop. Third, the statute places no termination date on the eavesdrop once the conversation sought is seized. This is left entirely in the discretion of the officer. Finally, the statute's procedure, necessarily because its success depends on secrecy, has no requirement for notice as do conventional warrants, nor does it overcome this defect by requiring some showing of special facts. On the contrary, it permits uncontested entry without any showing of exigent circumstances. Such a showing of exigency, in order to avoid notice would appear more important in eavesdropping, with its inherent dangers, than that required when conventional procedures of search and seizure are utilized. Nor does the statute provide for a return on the warrant, thereby leaving full discretion in the officer as to the use of seized conversations of innocent as well as guilty parties. In short, the statute's blanket grant of permission to eavesdrop is without adequate judicial supervision or protective procedures. . . .

It is said that neither a warrant nor a statute authorizing eavesdropping can be drawn so as to meet the Fourth Amendment's requirements. If that be true, then the "fruits" of eavesdropping devices are barred under the Amendment. On the other hand this Court has in the past, under specific conditions and circumstances, sustained the use of eavesdropping devices. [In *Osborn* v. *United States*] the eavesdropping device was permitted where the "commission of a specific offense" was charged, its use was "under the most precise and discriminating circumstances" and the effective administration of justice in a federal court was at stake. The States are under no greater restrictions. . . . Our concern with the statute here is whether its language permits a trespassory invasion of the home, by general warrant, contrary to the command of the Fourth Amendment. As it is written, we believe that it does.

The Court stopped short of saying no statute authorizing an eavesdrop or wiretap could ever be constitutional. But its emphasis on *Osborn* indicates that such a statute will have to limit its authority to the "most precise and discriminating circumstances" and that the need for the intrusion must be substantial. In *Osborn*, "the effective administration of justice in a federal court was at stake."

The New York law did not require that a particular conversation be described. In *Osborn*, the informer was authorized to record only a specific conversation. The New York law permitted the intrusion to continue for two months, or longer. In *Osborn*, the authorization referred to one conversation. In short, the Supreme Court seems to be saying that for purposes of the Fourth Amendment, a conversation is like a tangible thing. Its probable content must be identified, and it must be located in time and space. It must be connected by probable cause to a crime and the crime must be serious enough to justify the intrusion. If these conditions, among others, are met, the conversation may be seized. As the Court said, the authorization in *Osborn* was lawful because it "afforded similar protections to those that are present in the use of conventional warrants authorizing the seizure of *tangible* evidence" (emphasis added).

Justice Douglas concurred in *Berger,* but he believed that any warrant authorizing an eavesdrop would necessarily be unconstitutional. He said:

> A discreet selective wiretap or electric "bugging" is of course not rummaging around, collecting everything in the particular time and space zone. But even though it is limited in time, it is the greatest of all invasions of privacy. It places a government agent in the bedroom, in the business conference, in the social hour, in the lawyer's office—everywhere and anywhere a "bug" can be placed.
>
> If a statute were to authorize placing a policeman in every home or office where it was shown that there was probable cause to believe that evidence of crime would be obtained, there is little doubt that it would be struck down as a bald invasion of privacy, far worse than the general warrants prohibited by the Fourth Amendment. I can see no difference between such a statute and one authorizing electronic surveillance, which, in effect, places an invisible policeman in the home. If anything, the latter is more offensive because the homeowner is completely unaware of the invasion of privacy. . . .

In *Katz* v. *United States,* the petitioner's conversations in a public phone booth were overheard by an electronic listening and recording device attached to the outside of the booth. The taped evidence was admitted in court and the petitioner was convicted of transmitting wagering information by telephone. Initially, the Court rejected an analysis of the issue in terms of whether the phone booth was a protected area. The "Fourth Amendment protects people, not places," said the Court. "What a person knowingly exposes to the public, even in his own home or office, is [not protected]. . . . But what he seeks to preserve as private, even in an area accessible to the public, may be constitutionally protected." The Court then considered the requirements of precedent:

The Government contends, however, that the activities of its agents in this case should not be tested by Fourth Amendment requirements, for the surveillance technique they employed involved no physical penetration of the telephone booth from which the petitioner placed his calls. It is true that the absence of such penetration was at one time thought to foreclose further Fourth Amendment inquiry, *Olmstead* v. *United States* . . . *Goldman* v. *United States,* for that Amendment was thought to limit only searches and seizures of tangible property. But "[t]he premise that property interests control the right of the Government to search and seize has been discredited." Thus, although a closely divided Court supposed in *Olmstead* that surveillance without any trespass and without the seizure of any material object fell outside the ambit of the Constitution, we have since departed from the narrow view on which that decision rested. Indeed, we have expressly held that the Fourth Amendment governs not only the seizure of tangible items, but extends as well to the recording of oral statements, overheard without any "technical trespass under . . . local property law." *Silverman* v. *United States.* . . . Once this much is acknowledged, and once it is recognized that the Fourth Amendment protects people—and not simply "areas"—against unreasonable searches and seizures, it becomes clear that the reach of that Amendment cannot turn upon the presence or absence of a physical intrusion into any given enclosure.

We conclude that the underpinnings of *Olmstead* and *Goldman* have been so eroded by our subsequent decisions that the "trespass" doctrine there enunciated can no longer be regarded as controlling. The Government's activities in electronically listening to and recording the petitioner's words violated the privacy upon which he justifiably relied while using the telephone booth and thus constituted a "search and seizure" within the meaning of the Fourth Amendment. The fact that the electronic device employed to achieve that end did not happen to penetrate the wall of the booth can have no constitutional significance.

The Government argued, however, that the invasion of the petitioner's Fourth Amendment right was justified. The Court assumed that the

surveillance was so narrowly circumscribed that a duly authorized magistrate, properly notified of the need for such investigation, specifically informed of the basis on which it was to proceed, and clearly apprised of the precise intrusion it would entail, could constitutionally have authorized, with appropriate safeguards, the very limited search and seizure that the Government asserts in fact took place. . . .

The Government urges that, because its agents relied upon the decisions in *Olmstead* and *Goldman,* and because they did no more here than they might properly have done with prior judicial sanction, we should retroactively validate their conduct. That we cannot do. It is apparent that the agents in this case acted with restraint. Yet the inescapable fact is that this restraint was imposed by the agents themselves, not by a judicial officer. They were not required, before commencing the search, to present their estimate of probable cause for detached scrutiny by a neutral magistrate. They were not compelled, during the conduct of the search itself, to observe precise limits established in advance by a specific court order. Nor were they directed, after the search had been completed, to notify the authorizing magistrate in detail of all that had been seized. In the absence of such safeguards, this Court has never sustained a search upon the sole ground that officers reasonably expected to find evidence of a particular crime and voluntarily confined their activities to the least intrusive means consistent with that end.

In *Katz,* a particular conversation at a particular time and place was overheard. The "surveillance was so narrowly circumscribed" that it could constitutionally have been authorized. But because the FBI agents made the determination of probable cause for themselves, the eavesdrop violated the Fourth Amendment. *Katz* reaffirms the conclusions suggested by *Berger*: The Court is willing to permit "listening-in" if the conversation is located in time and place, its probable content is shown, and an impartial magistrate makes the initial determination of probable cause.

Justice White, concurring, thought the government did not have to obey the Fourth Amendment when "national security" was involved. But Justices Brennan and Douglas disagreed. They believed the Constitution applied regardless of the crime and that the Court should not "improvise because a particular

crime seems particularly heinous." The Court ruled that the
question was "not presented by this case."

Justice Harlan concurred and expanded on the Court's opinion. He agreed that "The Fourth Amendment protects people,
not places." But he continued:

The question, however, is what protection it affords to those
people. Generally, as here, the answer to that question requires
reference to a "place." My understanding of the rule that has
emerged from prior decisions is that there is a twofold requirement,
first that a person have exhibited an actual (subjective) expectation
of privacy and, second, that the expectation be one that society
is prepared to recognize as "reasonable." Thus a man's home is,
for most purposes, a place where he expects privacy, but objects,
activities, or statements that he exposes to the "plain view" of
outsiders are not "protected" because no intention to keep them
to himself has been exhibited. On the other hand, conversations
in the open would not be protected against being overheard, for
the expectation of privacy under the circumstances would be unreasonable.

This addition by Justice Harlan seems essential to the Court's
holding. It is not enough that the speaker expect his conversation to be private, but his expectation must be a reasonable
one.

Justice Black was the lone dissenter.

In view of the Court's indication in *Katz* and *Berger* that
listening-in is permissible only under "the most precise and
discriminating circumstances," examine title III of the 1968
Crime Control Act, a Congressional attempt to statutorily fulfill the *Berger* and *Katz* requirements.

The second section of that Act makes it a crime to eavesdrop or wiretap with an electronic, mechanical or other device.
It is also a crime to procure someone else to eavesdrop or
wiretap. Furthermore, the Act prohibits willfully disclosing or
using the content of a wire or oral communication which a

person knows or should know was acquired in violation of the Act.

The second section also contains several important limitations. It is not unlawful "for a person acting under color of law to intercept a wire or oral communication, where such person is a party to the communication or one of the parties to the communication has given prior consent to such interception." This continues the long-established exception requiring the speaker to take his chances. And a person not acting under color of law, who is a party to a conversation, or has the consent of a party to the conversation, can also intercept a communication "unless such communication is intercepted for the purpose of committing any criminal or tortious act in violation of the Constitution or laws of the United States or of any State or for the purpose of committing any other injurious act." This exception will permit a private person to have a telephone conversation and let another listen in. It will also allow a practical jokester (or perhaps an industrial spy or a private detective) to plant a microphone in one room and allow others to listen to a conversation with an unsuspecting third party. In fact, this exception allows complete invasion of conversational privacy if done with the consent of at least one party to a conversation, no matter how many other parties there may be. But, the exception ends if the interception is for criminal, tortious, or "injurious" purposes. Is "injurious" wide enough to eat up the exception?

Finally, a third exception permits the President to eavesdrop and wiretap at will if "national security" is involved. Evidently, "national security" is defined by the President.[8]

---

[8] Attorney General John Mitchell has asserted that the Executive has the power to eavesdrop and wiretap without prior judicial approval or regard to Fourth Amendment requirements when "national security" or "intelligence" is involved. It is an indication of the breadth of these terms that the Attorney General's statement was made as part of his refusal to supply the Chicago Seven defendants (charged with violating

The Act then goes on to:

1. prohibit the manufacture, transportation, or advertisement of devices primarily used to intercept conversations;

2. provide for the forfeiture of any such devices;

3. exclude from all courts, legislative bodies, and regulatory agencies evidence secured in violation of the Act; and

4. authorize federal and state law enforcement officers to eavesdrop and wiretap under certain circumstances.

The last provision concerns us most. The Act authorizes federal judges to permit a wiretap or eavesdrop on application of the Attorney General or one of his assistants. Similarly, the Act permits state law enforcement officers to intercept wire and oral communications if permission is granted by a state judge, on application of a district attorney or state attorney general, and if the intrusion is conducted under a state statute which conforms to the federal law. Furthermore, the federal Act limits the crimes whose seriousness will justify an intrusion. However, the list is extensive. Eavesdropping and wiretapping are permissible to secure evidence of the following federal offenses: espionage, sabotage, treason, riots, illegal payments to labor organizations, murder, kidnapping, robbery, extortion, bribery of public officials, transmission of wagering information, interstate transportation of stolen property, counterfeiting, buying, selling, or dealing in narcotic drugs, marijuana, or other dangerous drugs, and about a dozen other crimes. Intrusions are also permitted for evidence of virtually any state felony.

To secure an order authorizing an eavesdrop or wiretap, a

---

the federal antiriot act during the 1968 Democratic convention in Chicago) with transcripts of eavesdrops and wiretaps of their conversations. Thus, the terms "national security" and "intelligence" apparently include not only foreign nationals, but American citizens with radical political views. See *The New York Times,* June 14, 1969, p. 1, col. 5. The Supreme Court has so far refused to rule whether the Fourth Amendment applies to "intelligence" surveillance, and, if not, whether the scope of the intelligence area is as broad as General Mitchell would like it. *Alderman* v. *United States* 394 U.S. 165 (1969); *Giordano* v. *United States* 394 U.S. 310 (1969).

federal or state attorney must submit an affidavit, as he would if he were seeking a traditional search warrant. The affidavit must include:

a. the identity of the [officers making and authorizing the application];

b. a full and complete statement of the facts and circumstances relied upon by the applicant, to justify his belief that an order should be issued, including . . . (iii) a particular description of the type of communications sought to be intercepted . . . ;

c. a full and complete statement as to whether or not other investigative procedures have been tried and failed or why they reasonably appear to be unlikely to succeed if tried or to be too dangerous; and

d. a statement of the period of time for which the interception is required to be maintained. . . .

The issuing judge may order an eavesdrop or wiretap if on the basis of the affidavit he finds that:

a. there is probable cause for belief that an individual is committing, has committed, or is about to commit [an enumerated offense];

b. there is probable cause for belief that particular communications concerning that offense will be obtained through such interception;

c. normal investigative procedures have been tried and have failed or reasonably appear to be unlikely to succeed if tried or to be too dangerous; and

d. there is probable cause for belief that the facilities from which, or the place where, the wire or oral communications are to be intercepted are being used, or are about to be used, in connection with the commission of such offense, or are leased to, listed in the name of, or commonly used by such person.

The judge's authorizing order must specify:

a. the identity of the person, if known, whose communications are to be intercepted;

b. the nature and location of the communications facilities as to which, or the place where, authority to intercept is granted;

c. a particular description of the type of communication sought to be intercepted, and a statement of the particular offense to which it relates;

d. the identity of the agency authorized to intercept the communications, and of the person authorizing the application; and

e. the period of time during which such interception is authorized, including a statement as to whether or not the interception shall automatically terminate when the described communication has been first obtained.

The Act prohibits "interception of any wire or oral communication for any period longer than is necessary to achieve the objective of the authorization, *nor in any event longer than thirty days.*" (Emphasis added.) Unlimited extensions are permissible for periods of up to thirty days if a new, valid application is made and a judge makes the same findings required for the first authorization. The judge may require reports on the progress made toward "the authorized objective and the need for continued interception."

In an emergency, certain state and federal law enforcement officials may authorize a wiretap or eavesdrop without a court order if national security or organized crime is involved. The official must first determine whether or not judicial authorization would be granted if there were time to seek it. But even when an emergency intrusion is allowed, the federal or state officials responsible must seek a judicial authorization within forty-eight hours. Information obtained under this emergency provision is secured in violation of the Act unless judicial authorization is eventually received.

Finally, the Act generally requires that the authorities notify those persons whose names appear in the affidavit and any others the judge determines should be notified of the intrusion. This must be done within ninety days after the intrusion occurs. The Act also provides that a person who violates the Act, unless in reliance on a court order in good faith, is liable for damages to the "person whose wire or oral communication is intercepted, disclosed, or used in violation of this chapter."

The single most troubling provision of title III is the one that authorizes intrusions for periods up to thirty days. This seems a direct contradiction of the Court's requirement that the conversation to be seized must be particularly located in time and space. In *Osborn,* the authorizing judges permitted the agent to record a conversation, identified as to place and time, whose content would likely show that an officer of the court was attempting to bribe a juror. A valid statute could have authorized the intrusion in *Katz* because there was a particular conversation at a particular time and place and no others. There was ample cause to believe that the conversation would involve a criminal activity. But the 1968 Act permits the seizure of *all* conversations in a particular place, or on a particular phone, for up to thirty days (or longer) because it is likely that one or more of them, though not all, will provide evidence of a crime. What is absent is the substantial time limit, which was present in *Osborn* and *Katz.* In *Berger,* the sixty-day provision was held defective. Is there a real difference between thirty and sixty days?

Another troubling aspect of title III is that it permits "listening-in" if it will aid in the solution of any felony. Greater intrusions may be tolerated in certain cases than will be in others. For example, there is a greater societal interest in saving a kidnapped child than in retrieving a stolen car. The following statement by Justice Jackson, discussing searches of tangible objects, is equally applicable to eavesdropping and wiretapping:

If we assume, for example, that a child is kidnapped and the officers throw a roadblock about the neighborhood and search every outgoing car, it would be a drastic and undiscriminating use of the search. The officers might be unable to show probable cause for searching any particular car. However, I should candidly strive hard to sustain such an action, executed fairly and in good faith, because it might be reasonable to subject travelers to that indignity if it was the only way to save a threatened life and detect a vicious crime. But I should not strain to sustain such a roadblock and universal search to salvage a few bottles of bourbon and catch a bootlegger.[9]

Finally, Senator Philip Hart, a lawyer and a member of the Senate Judiciary Committee, dissented from the Committee's favorable report on title III. Consider his arguments which follow at some length:

> *Katz* involved that rare situation where electronic eavesdropping could be limited, not only with respect to time and place, but also to a specific person or persons and specific conversations. In *Katz*, FBI agents had established that Katz was in the habit of using certain public telephones at a certain location at a certain time to transmit wagering information. The FBI agents, therefore, installed a bug on the phone booth which was activated only when Katz entered the booth. The bug caught only Katz's end of the conversation and was turned off when he left.
>
> In approving this kind of eavesdropping, the Court emphasized that no conversations of innocent persons were overheard. It noted that "on the single occasion where the statements of another person were inadvertently intercepted, the (FBI) agents refrained from listening to them" (389 U.S. 347, 354). The Supreme Court placed particular emphasis on the extremely narrow circumstances under which the surveillance in *Katz* was conducted:
>
>> Accepting this account of the Government's actions as accurate, it is clear that *this surveillance was so narrowly circumscribed* that a duly authorized magistrate . . . clearly apprised of the precise intrusion could constitutionally have authorized, with appropriate safeguards, *the very limited search and seizure* that the Government asserts in fact took place (at 354). [Emphasis added.]
>
> *Katz* thus permits eavesdropping in one of the rare situations where it can be carefully circumscribed—a bug activated only when the suspect uses the "bugged" premises and recording only particular conversations of the suspect. Supreme Court approval of such

---

[9] *Brinegar* v. *United States,* 338 U.S. 160, 183 (1949).

a narrowly circumscribed eavesdropping situation as *Katz* does not imply approval of a thirty-day bug on a house or office (as is provided by title III), where many innocent people congregate to talk about many innocent things. . . .

The eavesdropping and wiretapping authorized by title III of S. 917, however, is essentially an indiscriminate dragnet. Section 2518(5) of title III authorizes wiretapping and eavesdropping orders for thirty-day periods. During such thirty-day authorizations, a title III bug or tap will normally be in continuous operation. Such a bug or tap will inevitably pick up all the conversations on the wire tapped or room bugged. Nothing can be done to capture only the conversations authorized in the tapping order. Thus, under title III, not only is the privacy of the telephone user invaded with respect to those calls relating to the offense for which the tap is installed, but all his other calls are overheard, no matter how irrelevant, intimate (husband-wife, doctor-patient, priest-penitent), or constitutionally privileged (attorney-client). Further, under title III all persons who respond to the telephone user's calls also have their conversations overheard. Likewise, under a title III tap, all other persons who use a tapped telephone are overhead, whether they be family, business associates, or visitors; and all persons who call a tapped phone are also overheard.

To illustrate the indiscriminate nature of a title III tap, one need only consider the experience of a New York police agent who in the course of tapping a single telephone recorded conversations involving, at the other end, the Julliard School of Music, Brooklyn Law School, Western Union, Mercantile National Bank, several restaurants, a drugstore, Prudential Insurance Co., the Medical Bureau To Aid Spanish Democracy, dentists, brokers, engineers, and a New York police station.

There is yet another fundamental inconsistency between title III and the requirements of the Constitution applicable to electronic surveillance, as interpreted by the Supreme Court in the *Berger* and *Katz* decisions. I believe that title III violates the requirement of these decisions that a warrant for electronic surveillance must particularly describe the conversations to be overheard.

As the Court emphasized time and again in *Berger* and *Katz*, the requirements of the fourth amendment applicable to wiretapping and eavesdropping are the same requirements applicable to conventional search warrants. Thus, it is clear that the overall purpose of *Berger* and *Katz* is to assimilate electronic surveillance to the strict requirements applicable to searches and seizures for tangible physical objects.

It has long been established that a conventional search warrant must describe with particularity the object to be seized, and that a judge authorizing the issuance of a warrant for the object must have probable cause to believe that the described object will be found on the premises to be searched. . . .

It is true that section 2518(3) (b) of title III requires a finding of probable cause for belief that particular communications concerning the offense named in the warrant will be intercepted. That provision, however, pays only lipservice to the constitutional mandate. The lengthy period of surveillance authorized in title III—up to thirty days, with unlimited renewals for fresh periods of thirty days each—belies the apparent adherence of title III to the requirement of particularity.

No one would suggest that a conventional search warrant may validly be issued to authorize a law enforcement officer to enter a private home or office and embark on a search lasting even a few days, let alone authorize the officer to move into the premises for a month.

Conventional searches lasting even a few hours have been roundly condemned in the courts as general, or "ransacking," searches. Yet it is precisely such a ransacking search that title III authorizes. A search lasting for a period of days or months can hardly be a search for a particularly described object. Unless we are to define "particularity" in novel terms, completely divorced from the requirements long held applicable to traditional search warrants, title III cannot stand.

Fortunately, the circumstances of the *Katz* case offer a clear example of what the Supreme Court intended as a valid application of the particularity requirement in existing search-and-seizure law to electronic surveillance. In *Katz,* the Federal investigating agents obviously had probable cause to believe that the particular communications made by the suspect from the public telephone booth were themselves part of the suspect's ongoing criminal activities. An application by the agents for a warrant authorizing the surveillance could clearly have described the communications to be intercepted with precisely the sort of particularity that is required in warrants authorizing searches for tangible physical objects.

The surveillance authorized by title III, however, is vastly different. It ranges far beyond the circumstances of *Katz*. Instead of requiring a meaningful description of particular communications to be intercepted, it authorizes all conversations of the person named in the warrant to be intercepted over the entire period of the surveillance, with law enforcement officers authorized to sift through the many varied conversations, innocent and otherwise, that take place during the period.

No search warrant could constitutionally authorize all of a person's future written statements to be seized for a thirty-day period, in the hope that one or another of the statements would contain certain incriminating information. The constitutional protection for oral statements can be no less. I suggest that no warrant should be able to authorize all of a person's conversations to be seized for a thirty-day period, in the hope that an incriminating conversation will be intercepted. Yet, this is precisely the sort of unlimited search contemplated by title III. It was not contemplated, nor is it permitted by the Constitution. . . .

Usually, one who opposes legislation in the belief it is unconstitutional opposes it also as unwise and undesirable. There is a chicken-egg question here, admittedly, and my opposition to legalizing wiretapping and eavesdropping goes beyond the constitutional doubts I have about title III.

Wiretapping and other forms of eavesdropping are recognized by even their most zealous advocates as encroachments on a man's right to privacy, characterized by Justice Brandeis as "the most comprehensive of rights and the right most valued by civilized men."

In yesteryear, a man could retire into his home or office free from the prying eye or ear. That time is now long past. Transmitting microphones the size of a sugar cube can be bought for less than $10. Other gadgets now enable a would-be snooper in New York to eavesdrop in Los Angeles merely by dialing a telephone number. This is done by attaching to the telephone in Los Angeles a beeper which converts the telephone into a transmitter without its ever leaving its cradle.

Directional microphones of the "shotgun" and parabolic mike type make it possible, by aiming the mike at a subject, to overhear conversations several hundred feet away. Laser beams permit an eavesdropper to monitor conversations in rooms up to half a mile away by aiming the beam at a thin wall or window. And the experts now tell us that in the years to come, as the methods of eaves-dropping technology surges forward, the problems of protecting personal privacy will even further intensify.

Against this backdrop of disminishing individual privacy, pro-ponents of title III now want to legitimate law enforcement wire-tapping and eavesdropping. Clearly, if such an effort is successful, today's narrowing enclave of individual privacy will shrink to the vanishing point.

6

THE RIGHT TO A LAWYER, APPOINTED OR RETAINED

The rules of criminal procedure are complex. In addition to the constitutional commands discussed in this book, there are numerous procedural and court rules to expedite the "business" of the criminal process. These vary from state to state. Also, rules of evidence differ in different jurisdictions. To a man charged with a crime, the assistance of counsel is essential. Government prosecutors are lawyers; they know the rules thoroughly. Defendants need equally well-trained legal assistance.

The Sixth Amendment guarantees that an "accused shall enjoy the right . . . to have the Assistance of Counsel for his defense." What does this guarantee encompass? This suspiciously simple question raises many problems. For example:

1. Does the right to counsel apply if an accused is unable to pay a lawyer? If so, how early in the criminal process must counsel be appointed? How long after conviction must counsel be provided? Is the penniless accused entitled to financial aid for a private investigator, expert witnesses, laboratory tests?

2. Does the right to the assistance of counsel apply in proceedings not labeled "criminal"—for example, probation revocation, habeas corpus, or other civil matters that might result in a loss of freedom?

3. Does the right to counsel apply in petty criminal cases? In misdemeanor cases? Does a defendant in traffic court who is charged with an illegal left turn have a right to counsel?

4. If the Sixth Amendment does not apply to petty cases, do the Due Process and Equal Protection Clauses require the state to supply indigents with counsel in all cases where defendants with funds might hire their own lawyers?

5. Does the Sixth Amendment's guarantee apply to the states, as well as to the federal government? If so, does it apply to them to the same extent?

6. What are the consequences if appointed counsel does an incompetent job in defending an accused?

The rich man doesn't have much trouble receiving Sixth Amendment protection. If a defendant has funds, there is an unqualified right to the assistance of counsel. This is true in both federal and state courts. *Chandler* v. *Fretag,* 348 U.S. 3 (1954) and *Ferguson* v. *Georgia,* 365 U.S. 570 (1961). The poor and middle-income man presents the problem. Today, the resolution of that problem may seem appallingly simple, but unfortunately the question troubled many judicial minds for a long time.

Powell v. *Alabama,* 287 U.S. 45 (1932), made a modest attempt to resolve the dilemma when it held that due process required the effective assistance of appointed counsel in a capital case involving "many complex issues" and "ignorant or feeble-minded defendants." Six years later, in *Johnson* v. *Zerbst,* 304 U.S. 458 (1938), the Court said an indigent defendant had a right to appointed counsel in federal criminal trials. The major question then became whether state courts were also obligated to appoint lawyers for indigents.

Many states, though not constitutionally compelled, did in fact provide attorneys to impoverished defendants either because their own constitutions required it or a state statute provided for it. Other states were less enlightened, and even those states that did provide counsel sometimes imposed preconditions

—the crime had to be of a certain variety or the defendant had to be totally without funds. Finally, in *Betts* v. *Brady,* 316 U.S. 455 (1942), the Court was asked whether state criminal courts were required by the federal Constitution to supply free counsel to indigents. The answer was no.

Betts is an unfortunate case because the Supreme Court and the defendant's lawyer framed the issue overbroadly. Betts was indicted for robbery, requested and was denied the assistance of appointed counsel, defended himself, lost, and received an eight-year sentence. The Supreme Court could have viewed the case as asking this question: Does the Sixth Amendment through the Due Process Clause require the appointment of counsel for an indigent defendant in a robbery case, or in felony cases generally? Instead the Court said the issue was whether "in every case, whatever the circumstances, one charged with crime, who is unable to obtain counsel, must be furnished counsel by the state." The Court said:

> [W]e are unable to say that the concept of due process incorporated in the Fourteenth Amendment obligates the states, whatever may be their own views, to furnish counsel in every . . . case. Every court has power, if it deems proper, to appoint counsel where that course seems to be required in the interest of fairness. . . .
>
> To deduce from the due process clause a rule binding upon the states in this matter would be to impose upon them . . . a requirement without distinction between criminal charges of different magnitude or in respect of courts of varying jurisdiction. . . . "Charges of small crimes tried before justices of the peace and capital charges tried in the higher courts would equally require the appointment of counsel. Presumably it would be argued that trials in the Traffic Court would require it." And indeed it was said by petitioner's counsel . . . that as the Fourteenth Amendment extends the protection of due process to property as well as to life and liberty, if we hold with the petitioner logic would require the furnishing of counsel in civil cases involving property.

Dissenting, Justices Black, Douglas, and Murphy believed the majority had drawn the issue too broadly. The question, said the dissenters, was whether "this petitioner" was denied his constitutional rights. The dissenters also believed the Fourteenth Amendment applied the full-strength of the Sixth Amendment to the states. They said: "A practice cannot be reconciled with 'common and fundamental ideas of fairness and right', which subjects innocent men to increased dangers of conviction merely because of their poverty." This palpably obvious statement could not win acceptance from a majority of the Court for twenty-one years; but in *Gideon* v. *Wainwright*, 372 U.S. 335 (1963), *Betts* was unanimously overruled. Excerpts from the Court's opinion in *Gideon* follow.[1]

Petitioner was charged in a Florida state court with having broken and entered a poolroom with intent to commit a misdemeanor. This offense is a felony under Florida law. Appearing in court without funds and without a lawyer, petitioner asked the court to appoint counsel for him, whereupon the following colloquy took place:

"THE COURT: Mr. Gideon, I am sorry, but I cannot appoint Counsel to represent you in this case. Under the laws of the State of Florida, the only time the Court can appoint Counsel to represent a Defendant is when that person is charged with a capital offense. I am sorry but I will have to deny your request to appoint Counsel to defend you in this case.

"THE DEFENDANT: The United States Supreme Court says I am entitled to be represented by Counsel."

Put to trial before a jury, Gideon conducted his defense about as well as could be expected from a layman. He made an opening statement to the jury, cross-examined the State's witnesses, presented witnesses in his own defense, declined to testify himself, and made a short argument "emphasizing his innocence to the charge contained in the Information filed in this case." The jury returned a verdict of guilty, and petitioner was sentenced to serve five years in the state prison. Later, petitioner filed in the Florida Supreme Court this habeas corpus petiton attacking his conviction and

[1] An interesting book about the Gideon decision is Anthony Lewis's *Gideon's Trumpet* (New York: Random House, 1964).

sentence on the ground that the trial court's refusal to appoint counsel for him denied him rights "guaranteed by the Constitution and the Bill of Rights by the United States Government." . . . To give this problem another review here, we granted *certiorari.* . . . Since Gideon was proceeding *in forma pauperis,* we appointed counsel to represent him.

The Sixth Amendment provides, "In all criminal prosecutions, the accused shall enjoy the right . . . to have the Assistance of Counsel for his defence." We have construed this to mean that in federal courts counsel must be provided for defendants unable to employ counsel unless the right is competently and intelligently waived. *Betts* argued that this right is extended to indigent defendants in state courts by the Fourteenth Amendment. . . . On the basis of . . . historical data the Court concluded that "appointment of counsel is not a fundamental right, essential to a fair trial." . . . It was for this reason the *Betts* Court refused to accept the contention that the Sixth Amendment's guarantee of counsel for indigent federal defendants was extended to or, in the words of that Court, "made obligatory upon the states by the Fourteenth Amendment." . . .

We think the Court in *Betts* had ample precedent for acknowledging that those guarantees of the Bill of Rights which are fundamental safeguards of liberty immune from federal abridgment are equally protected against state invasion by the Due Process Clause of the Fourteenth Amendment. This same principle was recognized, explained, and applied in *Powell* v. *Alabama.* . . . In many cases other than *Powell* and *Betts,* this Court has looked to the fundamental nature of original Bill of Rights guarantees to decide whether the Fourteenth Amendment makes them obligatory on the States. . . .

We accept *Betts* v. *Brady's* assumption, based as it was on our prior cases, that a provision of the Bill of Rights which is "fundamental and essential to a fair trial" is made obligatory upon the States by the Fourteenth Amendment. We think the Court in *Betts* was wrong, however, in concluding that the Sixth Amendment's guarantee of counsel is not one of these fundamental rights. . . .

The fact is that in deciding as it did—that "appointment of counsel is not a fundamental right, essential to a fair trial"—the Court in *Betts* v. *Brady* made an abrupt break with its own well-considered precedents. In returning to these old precedents, sounder we believe than the new, we but restore constitutional principles established to achieve a fair system of justice. Not only these precedents but also reason and reflection require us to recognize that in our adversary system of criminal justice, any person haled into court, who is too poor to hire a lawyer, cannot be assured a fair trial unless counsel is provided for him. This seems to us to be an obvious truth. Governments, both state and federal, quite properly spend vast sums of money to establish machinery to try defendants accused of crime. Lawyers to prosecute are everywhere deemed essential to protect the public's interest in an orderly society. Similarly, there are few defendants charged with crime, few indeed, who fail to hire the best lawyers they can get to prepare and present their defenses. That government hires lawyers to prosecute and defendants who have the money hire lawyers to defend are the strongest indications of the widespread belief that lawyers in criminal courts are necessities, not luxuries. The right of one charged with crime to counsel may not be deemed fundamental and essential to fair trials in some countries, but it is in ours. From the very beginning, our state and national constitutions and laws have laid great emphasis on procedural and substantive safeguards designed to assure fair trials before impartial tribunals in which every defendant stands equal before the law. This noble ideal cannot be realized if the poor man charged with crime has to face his accusers without a lawyer to assist him. . . .[2]

Gideon invoked the right to counsel at the trial level—but what about counsel on appeal? The Constitution nowhere requires a right of appeal, let alone appellate counsel. All states and the federal government do, however, have an appellate process. Recall that in *Griffin* v. *Illinois* (discussed in Chapter 2) the Court held that once the avenue of appeal is opened, its availability may not depend on wealth. Thus, in *Griffin,* Illinois was required to provide free transcripts to poor defendants who wished to appeal.

What about counsel on appeal? On the same day *Gideon* was decided, *Douglas* v. *California,* 372 U.S. 353 (1963), held that the constitution also required the states to give poor de-

---

[2] At his second trial, with the aid of counsel, Gideon was acquitted.

fendants free counsel on appeal. Unlike *Gideon,* however, *Douglas* does not rely on a Sixth Amendment right to counsel, but on a Fourteenth Amendment right to due process and equality. The Sixth Amendment only guarantees counsel at the trial level; the Fourteenth Amendment guarantees *equality* between rich and poor at the appellate level, if there is one.

The facts in *Douglas* were simple. Under California law, an indigent defendant who wished to appeal a conviction asked an appellate court to appoint counsel to aid him. The court would then investigate "the record and determine whether it would be of advantage to the defendant or helpful to the appellate court to have counsel appointed." In holding this procedure invalid, the Court noted that for the affluent defendant

the appellate court passes on the merits of [the] case only after having the full benefit of written briefs and oral argument by counsel.

For the poor defendant, however,

the appellate court is forced to prejudge the merits before it can even determine whether counsel should be provided.

The Court concluded:

There is lacking that equality demanded by the Fourteenth Amendment where the rich man . . . enjoys the benefit of counsel's examination into the record, research of the law, and marshalling of arguments on his behalf, while the indigent, already burdened by preliminary determination that his case is without merit, is forced to shift for himself. The indigent, where the record is unclear or the errors are hidden, has only the right to a meaningless ritual, while the rich man has a meaningful appeal.

The Court was careful to restrict its holding in *Douglas.* It noted that it was dealing with the first tier of appellate review and stated that it was not "here concerned with problems that might arise from the denial of counsel for the preparation of a petition for discretionary or mandatory review beyond the stage in the appellate process at which the claims have once been presented by a lawyer and passed upon by an appellate court." The Court also said that different treatment of rich and poor does not violate the Fourteenth Amendment "so long as the result does not amount to a denial of due process or an 'invidious discrimination.' "

A person convicted of a crime may also need an attorney in habeas corpus proceedings. Recall that an incarcerated person can institute such a proceeding if he believes he is being held in violation of law. Often a prisoner in a state institution will seek habeas corpus relief in federal court, claiming his state trial denied him certain rights guaranteed by the Constitution or laws of the United States. The Constitution does not require the appointment of counsel in habeas corpus proceedings. Courts generally consider the merits of the petitioner's case and assign a lawyer only if the petitioner might have a case. (This is strikingly like the procedure outlawed in *Douglas*.)

On the other hand, indigent habeas corpus petitioners are usually entitled to free transcripts. The law thus assures the indigent access to all the avenues open to the wealthy, but it only sometimes supplies the know-how (in the form of a lawyer). The prisoner must often become his own lawyer. This burden has been eased somewhat by the Supreme Court's decision upholding the right of "jailhouse lawyers" to aid fellow inmates. *Johnson* v. *Avery*, 393 U.S. 483 (1969). However, most prisoners probably prefer professional help if they can get it.

Occasionally, it happens that a prisoner whose conviction has been affirmed on appeal is, nevertheless, released in a subsequent habeas corpus proceeding. This fact supports the argument that at least one habeas petition should be with the automatic appointment of counsel. However, there comes a time when the denial of counsel is no longer "invidious discrimination." If a man has been found guilty, if his conviction was affirmed on appeal, if a first petition for habeas corpus relief has been denied, and if all these proceedings occurred with the aid of competent counsel, it is reasonable to require that successive petitions have some merit before the court must appoint an attorney. Even an affluent prisoner will not continue to pay a lawyer when his arguments have been rejected three times and there is no likelihood of future success. Must the government do more for a poor man?

The indigent may also seek aid other than counsel. For example, must the state supply chemists, ballistic experts, handwriting analysts, private detectives, accountants, and other skilled personnel if these are reasonably necessary to prepare a defense? The federal Criminal Justice Act does allow small sums for these purposes for indigent defendants; but most states provide nothing. A wealthy man charged with forgery will hire handwriting experts if he believes they will help win his case. A poor man should have the same assistance.

In an important case, the government will spend large sums of money investigating the facts. The federal government has the entire FBI at its disposal. A major trial may receive thousands of man-hours in preparation. Potential jurors are occasionally checked so the prosecutor will know whom to challenge peremptorily and who is likely to be sympathetic to his case. Experts with impressive credentials, with experience in countless trials, will be paraded before the jury to recite opinions supporting the defendant's guilt. Against this reservoir of money and talent, what can the poor—indeed, all but the affluent— defendant do? Many defense attorneys claim they would win more of their cases if they had the resources of the federal government behind them. This is an exaggeration, but there is a kernel of truth to it. The concept of proof beyond a reasonable doubt shrinks substantially when the state decides to direct its arsenal against an accused.

This does not mean that the state and federal government should not use all the legal means available to fight crime and convict criminals. Nevertheless, a trial is intended to be a mechanism for the determination of truth. It permits the trier of fact (judge or jury) to determine what happened. It does this most efficiently through an adversary system. Plaintiff and defendant, bound by rules of evidence, attempt to reconstruct a past event. The plaintiff presents his case and the defendant, through the powerful weapon of cross-examination, can test the persuasiveness of the plaintiff's witnesses. The process is then repeated with the roles reversed. The judge or jury must decide what the facts are and apply the law to these facts. This process is praised as an excellent method of truth-determination. The praise is justified in most cases. But when one of the parties to a trial is the United States, or any political entity, with a ridiculous superiority in money and power and a willingness to use it, the adversary system may be at the mercy of the prosecution.

A friend and former prosecutor believes this view is "naive." He argues that governments, especially local ones, simply do not prepare cases thoroughly or allocate adequate funds to prosecute them. He agrees, however, that there is an exception for "publicized cases."

It is true that the average criminal trial involves minimal government effort. I am speaking, however, about those cases in which the government does decide to do all it can to obtain a conviction. In these cases, though they may be relatively few, the great economic disparity necessarily threatens the ability to get a fair trial. Nor is this disparity lessened by the rule requiring the state to give the defense any exculpatory evidence it may have uncovered. The state does not conduct its investigation as a nonpartisan. The question is: Was the defendant as able as the state to conduct a thorough factual investigation and hire competent counsel? Almost always, the answer is no.

Gideon involved a felony—breaking and entering. Does the Sixth Amendment's guarantee extend to minor crimes? It does if the accused hires his own counsel, but is the indigent misdemeanant or petty offender entitled to an attorney? Seven years after *Gideon,* the answer to this question is still not known. The Supreme Court has yet to define the meaning of the words "criminal prosecutions" as used in the Sixth Amendment.[3]

If the Sixth Amendment does not guarantee counsel to minor offenders, might the Fourteenth? Recall *Douglas* and *Griffin.* Those cases relied on the Fourteenth Amendment's requirement of equal treatment to require counsel and a transcript on appeal. The same argument may be made for minor crimes: since an affluent misdeameanant is permitted to hire counsel, due process and equal protection should require that an indigent offender receive free assistance of counsel.

How far will this argument take us? For example, some persons might hire a lawyer to defend a littering charge. Must the state supply a lawyer for every poor litterbug? On the other hand, what if the offense is more serious—simple assault, punishable by up to six months in jail?

The answers to these questions do not depend only on legal considerations. There are simply not enough lawyers to defend every minor criminal charge. But even if there were, it is not invidious discrimination to require a poor person to contest his parking ticket without a lawyer. Most people who receive parking tickets or a summons for littering can afford a lawyer. Few, however, will pay $150 to defend a charge whose maximum penalty is $25. Should the state be required to do more for a poor defendant than common sense leads other defendants to do for themselves?

What should really concern us are the consequences of conviction. "Felony," "misdemeanor," and "petty offense" are labels we try to attach to different crimes according to the seriousness of each. But this triple division is arbitrary and far from

---

[3] In *Mempa* v. *Rhay,* 389 U.S. 128 (1967), the Court unanimously required appointed counsel at a probation revocation hearing. See also *In re Gault,* discussed in Chapter 8.

uniform. If the consequences of conviction are harsh, a defendant who can afford it will hire the best lawyer he can. If the consequences are insignificant—a small fine—few will hire an attorney. The state should be required to supply a lawyer only in those cases where the defendant, if he could afford it, would reasonably have hired a lawyer for himself.

The test should be objective. At what point are the consequences of conviction serious enough to require the state to provide an attorney to an indigent accused? Once we determine that point, we can return to the legal issue and define the Sixth and Fourteenth Amendments in terms of it.

The American Bar Association's Project on Minimum Standards for Criminal Justice suggests that counsel be provided for all offenses where loss of liberty is a practical possibility. The ABA suggests that the classification of the offense as felony, misdemeanor, or petty is irrelevant. Potential incarceration is the test.

The ABA approach is the least the Constitution should require. Counsel should be provided free, as well, in those cases where conviction may result in loss of livelihood. For example, a person whose living depends on his possession of a driver's license, such as a bus or cab driver, is arrested on a traffic offense. Conviction will result in suspension of his license, though not imprisonment. Such a defendant should also be provided with counsel if he is unable to afford one.

Gideon's requirement of free counsel will not be satisfied if the court-appointed attorney is incompetent. Since *Gideon,* cases have struggled with the meaning of "effective assistance" of counsel, and with the role of the court-appointed lawyer in his relationship with his client.

Courts are generally reluctant to invalidate a conviction if that decision requires a determination that the lawyer did not do his job. Frequently, courts will say that what appears to be an error only seems that way in retrospect; that the lawyer's

action in, for example, not objecting to a particular piece of
evidence may have been motivated by overall trial strategy,
which the court will not second-guess. Courts may also avoid
reversal by finding that the lawyer's mistakes were insignificant
and did not affect the determination of guilt. Decisions in this
area necessarily depend on the facts of the particular case.

An interesting collateral question concerns the rights of the
defendant who retains counsel. Should the standards of attorney competence be the same for him as for the indigent with
appointed counsel? Courts are less likely to reverse when retained counsel errs. Unlike the indigent, the defendant with
funds is considered free to choose his own lawyer. Therefore,
courts say, he is not as free to complain when his lawyer errs.
This argument is not convincing. A person with a moderate in-
come is not "free" to choose his own lawyer. In most cases, he
will retain the first lawyer whose office he stumbles into or
whom someone recommends on word-of-mouth.

In *Smallwood* v. *Warden,* 205 F.Supp. 325 (1962), a federal
district judge granted a petition for habeas corpus because the
defendant was not adequately represented by his court-appointed counsel. Smallwood, a Negro, was convicted in Maryland state court of raping a white woman. The court, in discussing the representation Smallwood received from his lawyer,
said:

Smallwood, a Negro oyster tonger with an eighth grade education, twenty-seven years old at the time of his trial, had been convicted several times by magistrates, but he had never been charged
with a sex offense nor tried in a court of general jurisdiction. On
December 6, 1956, he had sexual intercourse with a white woman
in a wooded area off a road in St. Mary's County, Maryland. A
co–defendant, who was with him, was found guilty of assault but
not guilty of rape. Smallwood has never denied having intercourse
with the woman, but has always denied using force, and claims that
she consented. . . .

Smallwood's lawyer saw him only twice before the trial. On the first occasion, March 19, the interview was brief; the lawyer recommended that the case be removed from St. Mary's County because of prejudice from the unfavorable newspaper publicity. Smallwood reluctantly agreed, partly because he was under the impression, apparently mistaken, that he could not get a prompt trial in St. Mary's County because of repairs being made to the Court House. Smallwood's lawyer did not ask him for a full statement at that time, and did not consider checking on the local reputation of the prosecuting witness before deciding whether the case should be removed. The suggestion of removal was filed the same day.

Two or three weeks later Smallwood's lawyer visited him at the jail and took a full statement from him, to the effect that the prosecuting witness drank with the defendants by the side of the road and had intercourse with Smallwood on the promise of money. Smallwood told his lawyer that a taxi-driver in a nearby cell knew about the reputation of the prosecuting witness for associating with Negroes and asked his lawyer to talk to the taxi-driver and to a tavern owner who had information which might help the defense. Despite the fact that the lawyer had the name of the taxi-driver and passed his cell on the way out, the lawyer made no effort at any time to interview him. The taxi-driver would have testified, as he did before me, that he worked the midnight shift, that on a number of occasions he had picked up the prosecuting witness and a colored man in the early morning hours, and that on two or three occasions she had had intercourse in his cab, once leaving unmistakable evidence thereof. Smallwood's lawyer did not interview any possible witnesses, made no preparation for the trial, and did not speak to Smallwood again until he was brought into court on April 29, in Charles County. The lawyer made no effort to obtain any information from the State, and the State's Attorney did not tell the defense or the court what he knew about the prosecuting witness.

Smallwood's lawyer made no adequate check on the prospective jurors, did not seek the assistance of a Charles County lawyer in selecting the jury, did not consider asking for a severance (although the State offered in evidence a verbal statement from the co-defendant implicating Smallwood, and the lawyer's only theory of defense was inadequate indentification), made no attempt to show consent or the reputation of the prosecuting witness, without discussing the problems with Smallwood decided not to put him on the stand, offered no evidence, made no requests for instructions, took no exceptions to the brief charge and asked for no further instructions, although the charge did not refer to the elements of the crimes charged nor to the burden of proof on the State. He did object to the offer of defendant's clothes on the ground that they had been illegally seized. His argument to the jury was not transcribed.

No timely motion for new trial was filed. The lawyer did not talk to Smallwood before the sentence hearing on May 22, and urged no facts in mitigation beyond saying that the former offenses had been of an entirely different nature. Smallwood said that he wanted to appeal, and one of the judges said that his court-appointed counsel would still represent him. On May 29, the lawyer asked for and was allowed $500 for his services in the Circuit Court.

The lawyer did not talk to Smallwood about the appeal and never told him that he had appealed or what the results were. About two weeks after sentence and commitment Smallwood wrote to the Court of Appeals saying that he wished to appeal, and was told by the Clerk that he was too late since the time limit was ten days. His counsel's appeal was filed several days later. His very short brief raised only the question of identification by the prosecuting witness; the illegal search and seizure point was not mentioned. . . .

The representation of Smallwood by his court-appointed counsel was so inadequate as practically to amount to no representation at all. The guarantee of due process was violated.

A simpler problem than effective assistance of counsel is the role of appointed counsel. Is court-appointed counsel's prime loyalty to the state, which pays him, or to the defendant? The short answer is that a court-appointed lawyer owes his client the same loyalty a retained counsel owes his. In *Anders* v. *California,* 386 U.S. 738 (1967), the defendant had sought to appeal his conviction for possession of narcotics. His appointed lawyer notified the appeals court that he believed there was no merit to the appeal. Anders' request for another lawyer was denied and he unsuccessfully appealed his own case. The Supreme Court (six to three) said the "no-merit" letter was an improper way to withdraw from an appeal that an appointed lawyer believes is frivolous.

The constitutional requirement of substantial equality and fair process can only be attained where counsel acts in the role of an active advocate in behalf of his client, as opposed to that of *amicus curiae*. The no-merit letter and the procedure it triggers do not reach that dignity. Counsel should, and can with honor and without conflict, be of more assistance to his client and to the court. His role as advocate requires that he support his client's appeal to the best of his ability. Of course, if counsel finds his case to be wholly frivolous, after a conscientious examination of it, he should so advise the court and request permission to withdraw. That request must, however, be accompanied by a brief referring to anything in the record that might arguably support the appeal. A copy of counsel's brief should be furnished the indigent and time allowed him to raise any points that he chooses; the court—not counsel—then proceeds, after a full examination of all the proceedings, to decide whether the case is wholly frivolous. If it so finds it may grant counsel's request to withdraw and dismiss the appeal. . . . On the other hand, if it finds any of the legal points arguable on their merits (and therefore not frivolous) it must, prior to decision, afford the indigent the assistance of counsel to argue the appeal.

Another question in the right-to-counsel area is the definition of "indigent." How poor must a defendant be before appointed counsel is supplied? He need not be entirely penniless. But if he has barely enough money to hire a lawyer, he may not get help. This result is inequitable. The defendant with $500 saved may be required to hire a mediocre lawyer, while his counterpart with $100 may get a better lawyer free. (Courts, particularly federal courts, are careful to supply indigents with good attorneys in order to avoid future claims of incompetence.)

There is another, less apparent but equally troubling inequity here. A middle-class defendant, who owns a car, a home, and has several thousand dollars in the bank clearly must hire his own attorney. The defense of a simple felony from arrest to trial may cost him $2,000 or more. If the case is complex, or if it involves a difficult legal issue, the cost may increase. If the defendant is eventually acquitted, it means the state could not prove him guilty beyond a reasonable doubt and, for legal purposes, he is innocent. But what about the attorney's fee? The acquitted defendant has been punished in a way that may hurt more than a small fine or jail sentence. He is not guilty but he is out thousands of dollars. Perhaps any person tried by the state without success should have all his costs reimbursed as a matter of right or at the discretion of the court and jury. This would include reasonable attorney fees as well as costs of investigation and fees for expert witnesses. In addition to the inherent fairness of this approach, it will induce innocent persons accused of petty crimes to see the matter through rather than succumb to the "realities" of the situation and plead to a lesser offense. The current theory is that litigants in civil and criminal cases are obligated to pay their own attorneys regardless of the outcome of the case.[4] Whatever the merits of this theory in civil cases, it is not persuasive in those criminal cases, at least, where the defendant is acquitted. The state was unable to get its man. The defendant should not have to suffer financially as a result of the state's unsuccessful prosecution.

A final issue to consider is at what point in the criminal process the indigent first becomes entitled to appointed counsel. The simple answer is: as soon as he needs one. The accused needs the aid of counsel at trial, but even before trial much can happen that will affect the ultimate determination of guilt or innocence. For example, pleas of insanity or motions to suppress evidence may be required long before trial. Furthermore, a crucial element in any criminal trial is swift investigatory work. If a lawyer is appointed too late, clues and evidence may dry up and the defendant will be at a great disadvantage. Prior to trial a defendant might confess, or admit certain facts damaging to his defense. He has a right to be silent and a lawyer may be necessary to assure the application of that right. Lawyers can also help to secure reductions in bail, enabling the accused to be free pending trial.

In *White* v. *Maryland,* 373 U.S. 59 (1963), the Supreme

[4] There are some exceptions for a limited number of civil cases.

Court made it plain that the right to counsel means the right to have counsel at all "critical" stages of the procedure. A critical stage is one where rights are preserved or lost, depending on the defendant's actions. The defendant is entitled to an attorney to help him plan strategy and a defense.

In *White,* the defendant, without counsel, pleaded guilty to murder at a preliminary hearing. In Maryland, a defendant may plead at a preliminary hearing, but his plea can later be changed. There are no motions that must be made at this stage or lost forever. In fact, White later did change his plea to not guilty by reason of insanity. What made the preliminary hearing critical, however, was the fact that the prosecutor was permitted to introduce White's guilty plea in evidence at trial. Thus, there was a very real consequence to White's unadvised action at his preliminary hearing—the jury learned he had once pleaded guilty to the crime for which he was then being tried. Since this critical plea was entered without the assistance of counsel, White's Sixth Amendment right had been violated and his conviction was reversed.

But the need for a lawyer arises even before the stage of the criminal process represented by the courtroom appearance in *White* v. *Maryland.* Since most people do not know the rules and since the police do, or should, know the limits of their power, most suspects cannot effectively assert their rights even at the initial stages of the criminal process. It is important therefore that a suspect receive the aid of counsel—or at least know he has the right to such aid—as soon after arrest as possible. Arrest, or custody, then, is the earliest critical stage. Many rights may be lost in the stationhouse. And, as we shall see in the next Chapter, today an accused is entitled to hire a lawyer, or if he cannot afford one, have a lawyer appointed for him, as soon as an investigation begins to focus on him—or, in the language of *Miranda* v. *Arizona,* as soon as he "has been taken into custody or otherwise deprived of his freedom in any significant way."

7

POLICE INTERROGATION AND
THE PRIVILEGE
AGAINST SELF-INCRIMINATION

Respect for constitutional rights in court will mean little if the same rights are not adequately protected during the pretrial stages of the criminal process. For example, the state may not, in court, question the defendant at length about the case; it may not even force him to take the witness stand if he chooses not to. But courtroom formality will be tokenism if, before trial, the police can question the suspect without check until he confesses and then use the confession at trial. In short, the adversary process begins before the parties ever see a courtroom. Constitutional protection is as fully required for the suspect at the early, informal stages of the process as at the later, formal ones.

On the other hand, the state must be able to investigate criminal activity, ask questions, follow leads. Imposing constitutional rules too early may result in unnecessary restrictions on the state's ability to solve and prevent crime. At what point, then, do the constitutional rules come into play? Where is the balance?

Federal Courts

For a long time, the federal courts have followed certain rules concerning admissions and confessions.[1] These rules are not required by the Constitution. The Supreme Court, as supervisor of the federal judicial system, has applied them to lower federal courts, but it has not held that the Constitution also applies them to the states. However, other cases, relying on constitutional interpretation, apply a different set of rules to state and federal courts. We shall first discuss the supervisory federal rules, and then the constitutional requirements.

In *McNabb* v. *United States,* 318 U.S. 332 (1943), the petitioners asked the Court to review their convictions for the murder of a revenue agent. When petitioners were arrested, a federal statute required the arresting officers to bring suspects before a judicial officer without delay. Petitioners were not taken before a judicial officer for several days and, in the interim, they confessed. The Court held that the confession should have been excluded from evidence. The federal statute did not specifically require exclusion of evidence secured in violation of its provisions, but the Court, exercising its supervisory powers over the federal system, believed exclusion was proper. Justice Frankfurter said:

The circumstances in which the statements admitted in evidence against the petitioners were secured reveal a plain disregard of the duty enjoined by Congress upon federal law officers. Freeman and Raymond McNabb were arrested in the middle of the night at their home. Instead of being brought before a United States Commissioner or a judicial officer, as the law requires, in order to

[1] A confession is a statement that the speaker committed a particular crime ("I killed Joe."). An admission is a statement which together with other proof shows that the speaker is guilty of a crime ("I own that gun, so what?"). I will use "confession" to refer to both confessions and admissions.

determine the sufficiency of the justification for their detention, they were put in a barren cell and kept there for fourteen hours. For two days they were subjected to unremitting questioning by numerous officers. Benjamin's confession was secured by detaining him unlawfully and questioning him continuously for five or six hours. The McNabbs had to submit to all this without the aid of friends or the benefit of counsel. The record leaves no room for doubt that the questioning of the petitioners took place while they were in the custody of the arresting officers and before any order of commitment was made. Plainly a conviction resting on evidence secured through such a flagrant disregard of the procedure which Congress has commanded cannot be allowed to stand without making the courts themselves accomplices in wilful disobedience of law. Congress has not explicitly forbidden the use of evidence so procured. But to permit such evidence to be made the basis of a conviction in the federal courts would stultify the policy which Congress has enacted into law.

Justice Stanley Reed dissented.

The *McNabb* rationale was undermined a year later when the Court, in *United States* v. *Mitchell*, 322 U.S. 65 (1944), intimated that mere delay in bringing an arrested suspect before a commissioner would not require exclusion of evidence. In *McNabb,* the *Mitchell* Court said, aggravating circumstances and psychological coercion required the result reached. For four years thereafter, *McNabb* was in doubt.

The confession in *Upshaw* v. *United States,* 335 U.S. 410 (1948), followed an unnecessary but pressure-free delay. The facts allowed the Court to decide just which view it wanted to take. The Court rejected its intimations in *Mitchell* and returned to the language in *McNabb*. Four Justices dissented.

The final case in this short but significant line of cases is *Mallory* v. *United States,* 354 U.S. 449 (1957). *Mallory* re-affirms *McNabb* and attempts to explain the type of delay that is prohibited. Mallory was arrested in the District of Columbia for rape. Although he was arrested at 2:30 P.M., he was not brought before a commissioner until the following morning and, in the interval, he confessed. The Court said:

The duty enjoined upon arresting officers to arraign "without unnecessary delay" indicates that the command does not call for mechanical or automatic obedience. Circumstances may justify a brief delay between arrest and arraignment, as for instance, where the story volunteered by the accused is susceptible of quick verification through third parties. But the delay must not be of a nature to give opportunity for the extraction of a confession.

The McNabb-Mallory rule is based on federal statute, not the Constitution. Congress can change the rule by changing the statute. It has done this in the same law that contained the wiretapping and eavesdropping provisions discussed in Chapter 5. Under the statute, voluntary confessions are admissible, although given during a period of delay, so long as the delay is shorter than six hours. Delays greater than six hours are excused if caused by transportation problems.

The next step in this area is the Court's. It will either accept the statute or, if it determines that the McNabb-Mallory rule is constitutionally required after all, invalidate the new law.

Constitutional Requirements

The second line of cases we deal with in this chapter relies on constitutional interpretation. These cases require the exclusion of confessions which (1) are not freely and voluntarily given, or which (2) are given during a period when the accused is denied his right to counsel, or which (3) are not preceded by certain warnings.

Freely and Voluntarily

Hogan in Chapter 3) grant a privilege against self-incrimination in criminal matters. In court, this means that a man may not be

The Fifth and Fourteenth Amendments (recall *Malloy* v.

forced to take the witness stand and give evidence against himself. But the privilege also means that the evidence a man is forced to give against himself outside the courtroom may not be used inside. In other words, the very introduction of a confession violates the Fifth and Fourteenth Amendments if the confession was not free and voluntary when it was made. A discussion of the cases in this area is essentially a discussion of the meaning of "freely and voluntarily." A man may decide to confess to a crime, but that decision must be his own. It cannot be the product of coercion.

A confession produced by physical torture is clearly coerced and inadmissible. *Brown* v. *Mississippi,* 297 U.S. 278 (1936). In *Brown,* the defendants were whipped with strap buckles and hung by their arms from trees. Coercion is also present when the suspect is denied food or sleep for long periods. In *Ashcraft* v. *Tennessee,* 322 U.S. 143 (1944), a conviction was reversed because the suspect confessed after thirty-six hours of continuous questioning. In *Leyra* v. *Denno,* 347 U.S. 556 (1954), the suspect, who suffered from a severe sinus condition, had been questioned in vain for two days. The police brought in Dr. Helfand, supposedly to help with the suspect's sinus problem. Actually Dr. Helfand was a psychiatrist and a hypnotist. After an hour and a half, the suspect confessed. The conviction was reversed.

In some of these cases, the confession is untrustworthy. But trustworthiness, though a consideration, is not the test. Was the confession voluntary; or was the mind of the confessor overborne by police tactics? The following excerpts from Supreme Court cases attempt to define "voluntary" and to explain the rationale underlying the Fifth Amendment.

This practice [of interrogation] has its manifest evils and dangers. Persons subjected to it are torn from the reliances of their daily existence and held at the mercy of those whose job it is—if such persons have committed crimes, as it is supposed they have—to convict them for it. They are deprived of freedom . . . without a proper judicial tribunal having found even that there is probable cause to believe that they may be guilty. What actually happens to them behind the closed door of the interrogation room is difficult if not impossible to ascertain. Certainly, if through excess of zeal or aggressive impatience or flaring up of temper in the face of obstinate silence, a prisoner is abused, he is faced with the task of overcoming, by his lone testimony, solemn official denials. The prisoner knows this—knows that no friendly or disinterested witness is present—and the knowledge may itself induce fear. But, in any case, the risk is great that the police will accomplish behind their closed door precisely what the demands of our legal order forbid: make a suspect the unwilling collaborator in establishing his guilt. This they may accomplish not only with ropes and a rubber hose, not only by relay questioning persistently, insistently subjugating a tired mind, but by subtler devices.

In the police station a prisoner is surrounded by known hostile forces. He is disoriented from the world he knows and in which he finds support. He is subject to coercing impingements, undermining even if not obvious pressures of every variety. In such an atmosphere, questioning that is long continued—even if it is only repeated at intervals, never protracted to the point of physical exhaustion—inevitably suggests that the questioner has a right to, and expects, an answer. This is so, certainly, when the prisoner has never been told that he need not answer and when, because his commitment to custody seems to be at the will of his questioners, he has every reason to believe that he will be held and interrogated until he speaks. [Justice Frankfurter in *Culombe* v. *Connecticut* 367 U.S. 568 (1961).]

The abhorrence of society to the use of involuntary confessions does not turn alone on their inherent untrustworthiness. It also turns on the deep-rooted feeling that the police must obey the law while enforcing the law; that in the end life and liberty can be as much endangered from illegal methods used to convict those thought to be criminals as from the actual criminals themselves. Accordingly, the actions of police in obtaining confessions have come under scrutiny in a long series of cases. Those cases suggest that in recent years law enforcement officials have become increasingly aware of the burden which they share, along with our courts, in protecting fundamental rights of our citizenry, including that portion of our citizenry suspected of crime. The facts of no case recently in this Court have quite approached the brutal beatings in

Brown v. *Mississippi* . . . or the thirty-six consecutive hours of questioning present in *Ashcraft* v. *Tennessee.* . . . But as law enforcement officers become more responsible, and the methods used to extract confessions more sophisticated, our duty to enforce federal constitutional protections does not cease. It only becomes more difficult because of the more delicate judgments to be made. [Chief Justice Warren in *Spano* v. *New York,* 360 U.S. 315 (1959).]

Our decisions under [the Fourteenth] Amendment have made clear that convictions following the admission into evidence of confessions which are involuntary, i.e., the product of coercion, either physical or psychological, cannot stand. This is so . . . because the methods used to extract them offend an underlying principle in the enforcement of our criminal law: that ours is an accusatorial and not an inquisitorial system—a system in which the State must establish guilt by evidence independently and freely secured and may not by coercion prove its charge against an accused out of his own mouth. . . . To be sure, confessions cruelly extorted may be and have been, to an unascertained extent, found to be untrustworthy. But the constitutional principle of excluding confessions that are not voluntary does not rest on this consideration. Indeed, in many of the cases in which the command of the Due Process Clause has compelled us to reverse state convictions involving the use of confessions obtained by impermissible methods, independent corroborating evidence left little doubt of the truth of what the defendant had confessed. Despite such verification, confessions were found to be the product of constitutionally impermissible methods in their inducement. Since a defendant had been subjected to pressures to which, under our accusatorial system, an accused should not be subjected, we were constrained to find that the procedures leading to his conviction had failed to afford him that due process of law which the Fourteenth Amendment guarantees. [Justice Frankfurter in *Rogers* v. *Richmond,* 365 U.S. 534 (1961).]

We cannot blind ourselves to what experience unmistakably teaches: that even apart from the express threat, the basic techniques present here—the secret and incommunicado detention and interrogation—are devices adapted and used to extort confessions from suspects. Of course, detection and solution of crime is, at best, a difficult and arduous task requiring determination and persistence on the part of all responsible officers charged with the duty of law enforcement. And, certainly, we do not mean to suggest that all interrogation of witnesses and suspects is impermissible. Such questioning is undoubtedly an essential tool in effective law enforcement. The line between proper and permissible police conduct and techniques and methods offensive to due process is, at best, a difficult one to draw, particularly in cases such as this where it is necessary to make fine judgments as to the effect of psychologically coercive pressures and inducements on the mind and will of an accused. But we cannot escape the demands of judging or of making the difficult appraisals inherent in determining whether constitutional rights have been violated. [Justice Goldberg in *Haynes* v. *Washington,* 373 U.S. 503 (1963).]

The concept of voluntariness, like all the concepts that the Court fashions, can only be explained in broad and general language. The facts of particular cases concretize the meaning of "voluntary." The situations noted above—prolonged denial of food or sleep, hypnosis—are clearly productive of involuntary confessions. Other techniques are less clear, more subtle. During the last fifteen years the Court has shown its awareness of these new techniques. The following cases illustrate the modern meaning of "voluntary."

The defendant in *Spano* v. *New York,* 360 U.S. 315 (1959) was convicted of murder and sentenced to death. Spano was a twenty-five-year-old immigrant who had dropped out of high school. He was drinking in a bar when the victim, a former professional boxer, took some of his money. Spano tried to recover the money, but the victim knocked him down and kicked him in the head. Spano got a gun, found the victim in a nearby candy store, killed him, and then disappeared for a week.

In the meantime, Spano was indicted. Still in hiding, he called Bruno, an old friend and rookie policeman. He told Bruno he wanted to get a lawyer and give up. The next day at 7 P.M. Spano, with his lawyer, surrendered to the district attorney. Spano's lawyer cautioned him to say nothing.

The interrogation began. Six officers questioned Spano for five hours without success. Spano asked in vain to see his lawyer. After midnight, Bruno was called. "Although, in fact, his job was in no way threatened, Bruno was told to tell [Spano] that [Spano's] telephone call had gotten him 'in a lot of trouble,' and that he should seek to extract sympathy from [Spano] for Bruno's pregnant wife and three children."

Bruno used this approach unsuccessfully. He was ordered to try again, but again he was unsuccessful. A third attempt also produced no confession. Finally, during a fourth try, Spano talked. It was now after 4 A.M. During the next few hours, Spano made additional statements. He was not brought before a judicial officer until after 10 A.M.

In reversing Spano's conviction the Supreme Court said:

Petitioner was questioned for virtually eight straight hours before he confessed, with his only respite being a transfer to an arena presumably considered more appropriate by the police for the task at hand. Nor was the questioning conducted during normal business hours, but began in early evening, continued into the night, and did not bear fruition until the not-too-early morning. The drama was not played out, with the final admissions obtained, until almost sunrise. In such circumstances slowly mounting fatigue does, and is calculated to, play its part. The questioners persisted in the face of his repeated refusals to answer on the advice of his attorney, and they ignored his reasonable requests to contact the local attorney whom he had already retained and who had personally delivered him into the custody of these officers in obedience to the bench warrant.

The use of Bruno, characterized in this Court by counsel for the State as a "childhood friend" of petitioner's, is another factor which deserves mention in the totality of the situation. Bruno's was the one face visible to petitioner in which he could put some trust. There was a bond of friendship between them going back a decade into adolescence. It was with this material that the officers felt they could overcome petitioner's will. They instructed Bruno falsely to state that petitioner's telephone call had gotten him into trouble, that his job was in jeopardy, and that loss of his job would be disastrous to his three children, his wife and his unborn child. And Bruno played this part of a worried father, harried by his superiors, in not one, but four different acts, the final one lasting an hour. Petitioner was apparently unaware of John Gay's famous couplet:

> "An open foe may prove a curse,
> But a pretended friend is worse,"

and he yielded to his false friend's entreaties.

We conclude that petitioner's will was overborne by official pressure, fatigue and sympathy falsely aroused after considering all the facts in their post–indictment setting. . . .

The *Spano* decision was unanimous. Perhaps because the pressure in *Haynes* v. *Washington,* 373 U.S. 503 (1963), was more subtle, only a bare majority of the Court concluded that the confession was not voluntary. Haynes was not denied food or sleep, but he was denied permission to call his lawyer or his wife. The police told him he could make no calls until he co-operated with them. He confessed after sixteen hours. He was nevertheless held incommunicado for five to seven days thereafter.

The Court held that secret and incommunicado detention was as likely to produce an involuntary confession as express threats or more overt psychological pressure. Haynes confessed under the apprehension that a refusal to do so would result in indefinite secret confinement, and his confession, therefore, was not voluntary. The Court made a point to note that Haynes was not informed that he did not have to speak. Nor was he told that anything he said could be used against him, nor that he had a right to an attorney. The failure to tell Haynes these things supported a finding of involuntariness. The Court did not yet say that these warnings were necessary, but the defendant's knowledge of these rights was part of the "totality of circumstances" a court should consider in determining voluntariness.

If we really do mean that a criminal suspect should not be forced to incriminate himself, the Court's rulings are understandable and unavoidable. To ignore the inherently coercive pressures on a person who has been cut off from friends and family and who is surrounded only by men whose job it is to make him talk is informally to deny what formally we guarantee. Criminologists have a variety of methods to make suspects talk. They argue that their methods will only make the guilty confess, not the innocent. Even if this is true, which is debatable, it is not the point. The state may not "make" anyone talk against himself. And a decision to talk is not free and voluntary if the pressures used to procure it are subtle rather than overt, psychological rather than physical.[2]

Right to Counsel

Statements may also be inadmissible because they were made during a period when the suspect was denied his right to counsel. The major cases in the area are *Massiah* v. *United States,* 377 U.S. 201 (1964), and *Escobedo* v. *Illinois,* 378 U.S. 478 (1964).

Massiah and *Escobedo* begin where Chapter 6 ended. In Chapter 6 we said that a criminal defendant's right to counsel attaches at the earliest critical state. In simple language, this means an accused has a right to counsel as soon as counsel can do him some good. If we are uncertain when that moment is, we might consider how long a suspect with enough money to hire a top criminal lawyer would wait. Indeed, an accused

[2] Perhaps the leading book in the confession area, written from the police viewpoint, is Fred E. Inbau and John E. Reid, *Criminal Interrogation and Confessions* (Baltimore: Williams and Wilkins, 1967). This book is a manual for police officers on the most effective methods to secure confessions from suspects. An excellent law review article, which discusses the concept of voluntariness and analyzes the methods advised by several police manuals, is Driver, "Confessions and the Social Psychology of Coercion," 82 *Harvard Law Review* 42 (1968). For an account of a major murder case where police tactics produced a false confession see Selwyn Raab, *Justice in the Back Room* (Cleveland: World Publishing, 1967).

has a need for the aid of counsel long before he ever sees the inside of a courtroom and, as this Chapter will soon make clear, he now has a right to counsel as soon as the "accusatory" process begins.

Massiah was indicted with a person named Colson and they were charged with conspiracy to import narcotics into the United States and with possessing narcotics aboard a United States vessel. Massiah pleaded not guilty, hired a lawyer, and put up bail. While Massiah awaited trial Colson offered to co-operate with the police. Colson's automobile was equipped with an eavesdropping device and Colson and Massiah had a conversation overheard by federal officials. Massiah made incriminating statements which were admitted in evidence at his trial. He appealed his conviction and the Supreme Court reversed.

The Court relied on the Sixth Amendment: "We hold [Massiah] was denied the basic protections of that guarantee when there was used against him at his trial evidence of his own incriminating words, which federal agents had deliberately elicited from him after he had been indicted and in the absence of his counsel." The indictment had been returned. The accusatory process had begun. The government could no longer collect evidence against Massiah from Massiah himself unless counsel was present.

Justices White, Clark, and Harlan dissented. They did not believe that government authorization of an informer to hold a conversation with Massiah violated the right to counsel. "Massiah was not prevented," they argued, "from consulting with counsel as often as he wished. No meetings with counsel were disturbed or spied upon. Preparation for trial was in no way obstructed. It is only a sterile syllogism—an unsound one, besides—to say that because Massiah had a right to counsel's aid before and during the trial, his out-of-court conversations and admissions must be excluded if obtained without counsel's consent or presence. The right to counsel has never meant as much before."

The dissent is correct: the right to counsel never did mean so much before. The *Massiah* extension reflects the decision by the Court that it is as important to safeguard rights before as during the trial. At the trial, Massiah could not have been forced to incriminate himself by a trick. If he had chosen to talk, that choice would have been made with the benefit of counsel. Likewise, he had a right to talk to his lawyer before incriminating himself to a government agent outside court.

It is important to the reasoning in *Massiah* that Colson was a government agent. If Colson had decided to cooperate after speaking with Massiah, the result would have been different. A defendant can furnish additional evidence of his guilt after indictment by freely speaking to everyone and anyone. But in this case, there was a government plan to make the defendant incriminate himself after his right to counsel had attached and the accusatory process had begun. This, the Court ruled, could not be done.

Danny Escobedo was denied access to his attorney after arrest, but, unlike Massiah, before indictment. While the police questioned Escobedo at the stationhouse, his lawyer entered and asked to speak with him. Though he made his request to several officers, Escobedo's lawyer was denied access to his client each time. Meanwhile, Escobedo asked in vain to see his lawyer. He later said the police told him his lawyer did not wish to see him. Eventually, Escobedo incriminated himself in his brother-in-law's murder and his statements were admitted at his trial. The Supreme Court, through Justice Goldberg, reversed the conviction, stating:

The interrogation here was conducted before petitioner was formally indicted. But in the context of this case, that fact should make no difference. When petitioner requested, and was denied, an opportunity to consult with his lawyer, the investigation had ceased to be a general investigation of "an unsolved crime." . . . Petitioner had become the accused, and the purpose of the interrogation was to "get him" to confess his guilt despite his constitutional right not to do so. At the time of his arrest and throughout the course of the interrogation, the police told petitioner that they had convincing evidence that he had fired the fatal shots. Without informing him of his absolute right to remain silent in the face of this accusation, the police urged him to make a statement. . . .

The "guiding hand of counsel" was essential to advise petitioner of his rights in this delicate situation. . . . This was the "stage when legal aid and advice" were most critical to petitioner. . . . It was a stage surely as critical as was the arraignment in *Hamilton* v. *Alabama* and the preliminary hearing in *White* v. *Maryland*. What happened at this interrogation could certainly "affect the whole trial," . . . since rights "may be as irretrievably lost, if not then and there asserted, as they are when an accused represented by counsel waives a right for strategic purposes." . . .

We have learned the lesson of history, ancient and modern, that a system of criminal law enforcement which comes to depend on the "confession" will, in the long run, be less reliable and more subject to abuses than a system which depends on extrinsic evidence independently secured through skillful investigation. . . .

We have also learned the companion lesson of history that no system of criminal justice can, or should, survive if it comes to depend for its continued effectiveness on the citizens' abdication through unawareness of their constitutional rights. No system worth preserving should have to *fear* that if an accused is permitted to consult with a lawyer, he will become aware of, and exercise, these rights. If the exercise of constitutional rights will thwart the effectiveness of a system of law enforcement, then there is something very wrong with that system.

Despite this broad language, the Court limited its holding significantly:

We hold, therefore, that where, as here, the investigation is no longer a general inquiry into an unsolved crime but has begun to focus on a particular suspect, the suspect has been taken into police custody, the police carry out a process of interrogations that lends itself to eliciting incriminating statements, the suspect has requested and been denied an opportunity to consult with his lawyer, and the police have not effectively warned him of his absolute constitutional right to remain silent, the accused has been denied "the Assistance of Counsel" in violation of the Sixth Amendment to the

Constitution . . . and that no statement elicited by the police during the interrogation may be used against him at a criminal trial.

Justice Stewart (with Justices Clark, Harlan and White) dissented. Justice Stewart had written the majority opinion in *Massiah,* but he did not believe that case inevitably led to *Escobedo.* He argued that Escobedo's right to counsel had not attached because he had not been indicted. But if indictment is the crucial act that attaches the right to counsel, the state could delay the right by delaying indictment. The right to counsel must attach when it is needed. It is needed, at the very least, as soon as the investigation has "begun to focus on a particular suspect" and he is in custody. Since the police did not allow Escobedo access to his lawyer during a period while the right to counsel was in force, statements elicited from the defendant during that period were inadmissible.

Miranda: Necessary Warnings

The *Massiah-Escobedo* addition to the *Spano-Haynes* test of voluntariness raised additional questions. For example, what if a suspect who has an attorney does not think to ask for him as Danny Escobedo did? What of the suspect who insists on an attorney but does not happen to have one in the stationhouse waiting to see him? Or, what if a suspect does not ask for a lawyer because he cannot afford one and does not know he is entitled to one for free?

The questions were answered, to some extent, in *Miranda* v. *Arizona,* 384 U.S. 436 (1966).[3] The Court shifted its focus (as well as its underlying rationale) from the Sixth Amendment's right to counsel to the Fifth Amendment's privilege

[3] Some commentators believe *Escobedo* is made obsolete by *Miranda* because a fact situation is not likely to arise that violates the first case and not the second. Whether this is true, *Escobedo* is still good law and will be around if anything happens to *Miranda.*

against self-incrimination, but it is still concerned with pretrial rights in an accusatory criminal process.

In effect, the *Miranda* Court said that all in-custody interrogation is inherently coercive and certain warnings are necessary to satisfactorily reduce the coercive atmosphere. If a suspect insists on the rights contained in the warning, the questioning must stop and the rights must be provided. Extensive excerpts from Chief Justice Warren's opinion in *Miranda* follow.[4]

The cases before us raise questions which go to the roots of our concepts of American criminal jurisprudence: the restraints society must observe consistent with the Federal Constitution in prosecuting individuals for crime. More specifically, we deal with the admissibility of statements obtained from an individual who is subjected to custodial police interrogation and the necessity for procedures which assure that the individual is accorded his privilege under the Fifth Amendment to the Constitution not to be compelled to incriminate himself. . . .

Our holding will be spelled out with some specificity in the pages which follow but briefly stated it is this: the prosecution may not use statements, whether exculpatory or inculpatory, stemming from custodial interrogation of the defendant unless it demonstrates the use of procedural safeguards effective to secure the privilege against self-incrimination. By custodial interrogation, we mean questioning initiated by law enforcement officers after a person has been taken into custody or otherwise deprived of his freedom of action in any significant way.* As for the procedural safeguards to be employed, unless other fully effective means are devised to inform accused persons of their right of silence and to assure a continuous opportunity to exercise it, the following measures are required. Prior to any questioning, the person must be warned that he has a right to remain silent, that any statement he does make may be used as evidence against him, and that he has a right to the presence of an attorney, either retained or appointed. The defendant may waive effectuation of these rights, provided the waiver is made voluntarily, knowingly and intelligently. If, however, he indicates in

---

4 Under the heading of *Miranda* v. *Arizona,* the Court actually decided four separate cases.

* This is what we meant in *Escobedo* when we spoke of an investigation which had focused on an accused.

any manner and at any stage of the process that he wishes to consult with an attorney before speaking there can be no questioning. Likewise, if the individual is alone and indicates in any manner that he does not wish to be interrogated, the police may not question him. The mere fact that he may have answered some questions or volunteered some statements on his own does not deprive him of the right to refrain from answering any further inquiries until he has consulted with an attorney and thereafter consents to be questioned.

The constitutional issue we decide in each of these cases is the admissibility of statements obtained from a defendant questioned while in custody and deprived of his freedom of action. In each, the defendant was questioned by police officers, detectives, or a prosecuting attorney in a room in which he was cut off from the outside world. In none of these cases was the defendant given a full and effective warning of his rights at the outset of the interrogation process. In all the cases, the questioning elicited oral admissions, and in three of them, signed statements as well which were admitted at their trials. They all thus share salient features—incommunicado interrogation of individuals in a police-dominated atmosphere, resulting in self-incriminating statements without full warnings of constitutional rights.

Again we stress that the modern practice of in-custody interrogation is psychologically rather than physically oriented. . . . Interrogation still takes place in privacy. Privacy results in secrecy and this in turn results in a gap in our knowledge as to what in fact goes on in the interrogation rooms. A valuable source of information about present police practices, however, may be found in various police manuals and texts which document procedures employed with success in the past, and which recommend various other effective tactics. These texts are used by law enforcement agencies themselves as guides. It should be noted that these texts professedly present the most enlightened and effective means presently used to obtain statements through custodial interrogation. By considering these texts and other data, it is possible to describe procedures observed and noted around the country.

The officers are told by the manuals that the "principal psychological factor contributing to a successful interrogation is *privacy* —being alone with the person under interrogation." The efficacy of this tactic has been explained as follows:

"If at all practicable, the interrogation should take place in the investigator's office or at least in a room of his own choice. The subject should be deprived of every psychological advantage. In his own home he may be confident, indignant, or recalcitrant. He is more keenly aware of his rights and more reluctant to tell of his indiscretions of criminal behavior within the walls of his own home. Moreover his family and other friends are nearby, their presence lending moral support. In his own office, the investigator possesses all the advantages. The atmosphere suggests the invincibility of the forces of the law."

To highlight the isolation and unfamiliar surroundings, the manuals instruct the police to display an air of confidence in the suspect's guilt and from outward appearance to maintain only an interest in confirming certain details. The guilt of the subject is to be posited as a fact. The interrogator should direct his comments toward the reasons why the subject committed the act, rather than to court failure by asking the subject whether he did it. Like other men, perhaps the subject has had a bad family life, had an unhappy childhood, had too much to drink, had an unrequited attraction to women. The officers are instructed to minimize the moral seriousness of the offense, to cast blame on the victim or on society. These tactics are designed to put the subject in a psychological state where his story is but an elaboration of what the police purport to know already—that he is guilty. Explanations to the contrary are dismissed and discouraged.

The texts thus stress that the major qualities an interrogator should possess are patience and perseverance. . . .

When the techniques described above prove unavailing, the texts recommend they be alternated with a show of some hostility. One ploy often used has been termed the "friendly-unfriendly" or the "Mutt and Jeff" act:

". . . In this technique, two agents are employed, Mutt, the relentless investigator, who knows the subject is guilty and is not going to waste any time. He's sent a dozen men away for this crime and he's going to send the subject away for the full term. Jeff, on the other hand, is obviously a kind-hearted man. He has a family himself. He has a brother who was involved in a little scrape like this. He disapproves of Mutt and his tactics and will arrange to get him off the case if the subject will cooperate. He can't hold Mutt off for very long. The subject would be wise to make a quick decision. The technique is applied by having both investigators present while Mutt acts out his role. Jeff may stand by quietly and demur at some of Mutt's tactics. When Jeff makes his plea for cooperation, Mutt is not present in the room."

The interrogators sometimes are instructed to induce a confession out of trickery. The technique here is quite effective in crimes which require identification or which run in series. In the identification situation, the interrogator may take a break in his questioning to place the subject among a group of men in a line-up. "The witness or complainant (previously coached, if necessary) studies the line-up and confidently points out the subject as the guilty party." Then the questioning resumes "as though there were now no doubt about the guilt of the subject." A variation on this technique is called the "reverse line-up":

"The accused is placed in a line-up, but this time he is identified by several fictitious witnesses or victims who associated him with different offenses. It is expected that the subject will become desperate and confess to the offense under investigation in order to escape from the false accusations."

The manuals also contain instructions for police on how to handle the individual who refuses to discuss the matter entirely, or who asks for an attorney or relatives. The examiner is to concede him the right to remain silent. "This usually has a very undermining effect. First of all, he is disappointed in his expectation of an unfavorable reaction on the part of the interrogator. Secondly, a concession of this right to remain silent impresses the subject with the apparent fairness of his interrogator." After this psychological conditioning, however, the officer is told to point out the incriminating significance of the suspect's refusal to talk:

"Joe, you have a right to remain silent. That's your privilege and I'm the last person in the world who'll try to take it away from you. If that's the way you want to leave this, O. K. But let me ask you this. Suppose you were in my shoes and I were in yours and you called me in to ask me about this and I told you, 'I don't want to answer any of your questions.' You'd think I had something to hide, and you'd probably be right in thinking that. That's exactly what I'll have to think about you, and so will everybody else. So let's sit here and talk this whole thing over."

Few will persist in their initial refusals to talk, it is said, if this monologue is employed correctly.

In the event that the subject wishes to speak to a relative or an attorney, the following advice is tendered:

"[T]he interrogator should respond by suggesting the subject first tell the truth to the interrogator himself rather than get anyone else involved in the matter. If the request is for an attorney, the interrogator may suggest that the subject save himself or his family the expense of any such professional service, particularly if he is innocent of the offense under investigation. The interrogator may also add, 'Joe, I'm only looking for the truth, and if you're telling the truth, that's it. You can handle this by yourself.' "

From these representative samples of interrogation techniques, the setting prescribed by the manuals and observed in practice becomes clear. In essence, it is this: To be alone with the subject is essential to prevent distraction and to deprive him of any outside support. The aura of confidence in his guilt undermines his will to resist. He merely confirms the preconceived story the police seek to have him describe. Patience and persistence, at times relentless questioning, are employed. To obtain a confession, the interrogator must "patiently maneuver himself or his quarry into a position from which the desired object may be obtained." When normal procedures fail to produce the needed result, the police may resort to deceptive stratagems such as giving false legal advice. It is important to keep the subject off balance, for example, by trading on his insecurity about himself or his surroundings. The police then persuade, trick, or cajole him out of exercising his constitutional rights.

Even without employing brutality, the "third degree" or the specific stratagems described above, the very fact of custodial interrogation exacts a heavy toll on individual liberty and trades on the weakness of individuals. . . .

In the cases before us today, given this background, we concern ourselves primarily with this interrogation atmosphere and the evils it can bring. . . .

In these cases, we might not find the defendants' statements to have been involuntary in traditional terms. Our concern for adequate safeguards to protect precious Fifth Amendment rights is, of course, not lessened in the slightest. In each of the cases, the defendant was thrust into an unfamiliar atmosphere and run through menacing police interrogation procedures. The potentiality for compulsion is forcefully apparent, for example, in *Miranda,* where the indigent Mexican defendant was a seriously disturbed individual with pronounced sexual fantasies, and in *Stewart,* in which the defendant was an indigent Los Angeles Negro who had dropped out of school in the sixth grade. To be sure, the records do not evince overt physical coercion or patented psychological ploys. The fact remains that in none of these cases did the officers undertake to afford appropriate safeguards at the outset of the interrogation to insure that the statements were truly the product of free choice.

It is obvious that such an interrogation environment is created for no purpose other than to subjugate the individual to the will of his examiner. This atmosphere carries its own badge of intimidation. To be sure, this is not physical intimidation, but it is equally destructive of human dignity.* The current practice of incommunicado interrogation is at odds with one of our Nation's most cherished principles—that the individual may not be compelled to incriminate himself. Unless adequate protective devices are employed to dispel the compulsion inherent in custodial surroundings, no statement obtained from the defendant can truly be the product of his free choice. . . .

---

* The absurdity of denying that a confession obtained under these circumstances is compelled is aptly portrayed by an example in Professor Sutherland's recent article, "Crime and Confession," 79 *Harvard Law Review* 21, 37 (1965).

"Suppose a well-to-do testatrix says she intends to will her property to Elizabeth. John and James want her to bequeath it to them instead. They capture the testatrix, put her in a carefully designed room, out of touch with everyone but themselves and their convenient 'witnesses,' keep her secluded there for hours while they make insistent demands, weary her with contradictions and finally induce her to execute the will in their favor. Assume that John and James are deeply and correctly convinced that Elizabeth is unworthy and will make base use of the property if she gets her hands on it, whereas John and James have the noblest and most righteous intentions. Would any judge of probate accept the will so procured as the 'voluntary' act of the testatrix?"

Today, then, there can be no doubt that the Fifth Amendment
privilege is available outside of criminal court proceedings and
serves to protect persons in all settings in which their freedom of
action is curtailed from being compelled to incriminate themselves.
We have concluded that without proper safeguards the process of
in-custody interrogation of persons suspected or accused of crime
contains inherently compelling pressures which work to undermine
the individual's will to resist and to compel him to speak where he
would not otherwise do so freely. In order to combat these pressures
and to permit a full opportunity to exercise the privilege against
self-incrimination, the accused must be adequately and effectively
apprised of his rights and the exercise of those rights must be fully
honored.

It is impossible for us to foresee the potential alternatives for protecting the privilege which might be devised by Congress or the
States in the exercise of their creative rule-making capacities. Therefore we cannot say that the Constitution necessarily requires adherence to any particular solution for the inherent compulsions of
the interrogation process as it is presently conducted. Our decision
in no way creates a constitutional straitjacket which will handicap
sound efforts at reform, nor is it intended to have this effect. We encourage Congress and the States to continue their laudable search
for increasingly effective ways of protecting the rights of the individual while promoting efficient enforcement of our criminal laws.
However, unless we are shown other procedures which are at least
as effective in apprising accused persons of their right of silence
and in assuring a continuous opportunity to exercise it, the following
safeguards must be observed.

At the outset, if a person in custody is to be subjected to interrogation, he must be first informed in clear and unequivocal terms that
he has the right to remain silent. For those unaware of the privilege,
the warning is needed simply to make them aware of it—the
threshold requirement for an intelligent decision as to its exercise.
More important, such a warning is an absolute prerequisite in overcoming the inherent pressures of the interrogation atmosphere. It is
not just the subnormal or woefully ignorant who succumb to an
interrogator's imprecations, whether implied or expressly stated,
that the interrogation will continue until a confession is obtained
or that silence in the face of accusation is itself damning and will

bode ill when presented to a jury. Further, the warning will show the individual that his interrogators are prepared to recognize his privilege should he choose to exercise it. . . .

The warning of the right to remain silent must be accompanied by the explanation that anything said can and will be used against the individual in court. This warning is needed in order to make him aware not only of the privilege, but also of the consequences of forgoing it. It is only through an awareness of these consequences that there can be any assurance of real understanding and intelligent exercise of the privilege. Moreover, this warning may serve to make the individual more acutely aware that he is faced with a phase of the adversary system—that he is not in the presence of persons acting solely in his interest.

The circumstances surrounding in-custody interrogation can operate very quickly to overbear the will of one merely made aware of his privilege by his interrogators. Therefore, the right to have counsel present at the interrogation is indispensable to the protection of the Fifth Amendment privilege under the system we delineate today. Our aim is to assure that the individual's right to choose between silence and speech remains unfettered throughout the interrogation process. A once-stated warning, delivered by those who will conduct the interrogation, cannot itself suffice to that end among those who most require knowledge of their rights. A mere warning given by the interrogators is not alone sufficient to accomplish that end. Prosecutors themselves claim that the admonishment of the right to remain silent without more "will benefit only the recidivist and the professional." . . . Even preliminary advice given to the accused by his own attorney can be swiftly overcome by the secret interrogation process. . . . Thus, the need for counsel to protect the Fifth Amendment privilege comprehends not merely a right to consult with counsel prior to questioning, but also to have counsel present during any questioning if the defendant so desires.

The presence of counsel at the interrogation may serve several significant subsidiary functions as well. If the accused decides to talk to his interrogators, the assistance of counsel can mitigate the dangers of untrustworthiness. With a lawyer present the likelihood that the police will practice coercion is reduced, and if coercion is nevertheless exercised the lawyer can testify to it in court. The presence of a lawyer can also help to guarantee that the accused gives a fully accurate statement to the police and that the statement is rightly reported by the prosecution at trial. . . .

An individual need not make a pre-interrogation request for a lawyer. While such request affirmatively secures his right to have one, his failure to ask for a lawyer does not constitute a waiver. No effective waiver of the right to counsel during interrogation can be recognized unless specifically made after the warnings we here delineate have been given. The accused who does not know his rights and therefore does not make a request may be the person who most needs counsel. . . .

Accordingly we hold that an individual held for interrogation must be clearly informed that he has the right to consult with a lawyer and to have the lawyer with him during interrogation under the system for protecting the privilege we delineate today. As with the warnings of the right to remain silent and that anything stated can be used in evidence against him, this warning is an absolute prerequisite to interrogation. No amount of circumstantial evidence that the person may have been aware of this right will suffice to stand in its stead. Only through such a warning is there ascertainable assurance that the accused was aware of this right.

If an individual indicates that he wishes the assistance of counsel before any interrogation occurs, the authorities cannot rationally ignore or deny his request on the basis that the individual does not have or cannot afford a retained attorney. The financial ability of the individual has no relationship to the scope of the rights involved here. The privilege against self-incrimination secured by the Constitution applies to all individuals. The need for counsel in order to protect the privilege exists for the indigent as well as the affluent. In fact, were we to limit these constitutional rights to those who can retain an attorney, our decisions today would be of little significance. The cases before us as well as the vast majority of confession cases with which we have dealt in the past involve those unable to retain counsel. While authorities are not required to relieve the accused of his poverty, they have the obligation not to take advantage of indigence in the administration of justice. Denial of counsel to the indigent at the time of interrogation while allowing an attorney to those who can afford one would be no more supportable by reason or logic than the similar situation at trial and on appeal struck down in *Gideon* v *Wainwright* . . . and *Douglas* v *California*. . . .

In order fully to apprise a person interrogated of the extent of his rights under this system then, it is necessary to warn him not only that he has the right to consult with an attorney, but also that if he is indigent a lawyer will be appointed to represent him. Without this additional warning, the admonition of the right to consult with counsel would often be understood as meaning only that he can consult with a lawyer if he has one or has the funds to obtain one. The warning of a right to counsel would be hollow if not couched in terms that would convey to the indigent—the person most often subjected to interrogation—the knowledge that he too has a right to have counsel present. As with the warnings of the right to remain silent and of the general right to counsel, only by effective and express explanation to the indigent of this right can there be assurance that he was truly in a position to exercise it.

Once warnings have been given, the subsequent procedure is clear. If the individual indicates in any manner, at any time prior to or during questioning, that he wishes to remain silent, the interrogation must cease. At this point he has shown that he intends to exercise his Fifth Amendment privilege; any statement taken after the person invokes his privilege cannot be other than the product of compulsion, subtle or otherwise. Without the right to cut off questioning, the setting of in-custody interrogation operates on the individual to overcome free choice in producing a statement after the privilege has been once invoked. If the individual states that he wants an attorney, the interrogation must cease until an attorney is present. At that time, the individual must have an opportunity to confer with the attorney and to have him present during any subsequent questioning. If the individual cannot obtain an attorney and he indicates that he wants one before speaking to police, they must respect his decision to remain silent. . . .

If the interrogation continues without the presence of an attorney and a statement is taken, a heavy burden rests on the Government to demonstrate that the defendant knowingly and intelligently waived his privilege against self-incrimination and his right to retained or appointed counsel. . . . This Court has always set high standards of proof for the waiver of constitutional rights . . . and we re-assert these standards as applied to in-custody interrogation. Since the State is responsible for establishing the isolated circumstances under which the interrogation takes place and has the only means of making available corroborated evidence of warnings given during incommunicado interrogation, the burden is rightly on its shoulders. . . .

The principles announced today deal with the protection which must be given to the privilege against self-incrimination when the individual is first subjected to police interrogation while in custody at the station or otherwise deprived of his freedom of action in any way. It is at this point that our adversary system of criminal proceedings commences, distinguishing itself at the outset from the inquisitorial system recognized in some countries. Under the system of warnings we delineate today or under any other system which may be devised and found effective, the safeguards to be erected about the privilege must come into play at this point.

Our decision is not intended to hamper the traditional function of police officers in investigating crime. . . . When an individual is in custody on probable cause, the police may, of course, seek out evidence in the field to be used at trial against him. Such investigation may include inquiry of persons not under restraint. General on-the-scene questioning as to facts surrounding a crime or other general questioning of citizens in the fact-finding process is not affected by our holding. It is an act of responsible citizenship for individuals to give whatever information they may have to aid in law enforcement. In such situations the compelling atmosphere inherent in the process of in-custody interrogation is not necessarily present.

In dealing with statements obtained through interrogation, we do not purport to find all confessions inadmissible. Confessions remain a proper element in law enforcement. Any statement given freely and voluntarily without any compelling influences is, of course, admissible in evidence. The fundamental import of the privilege while an individual is in custody is not whether he is allowed to talk to the police without the benefit of warnings and counsel, but whether he can be interrogated. There is no requirement that police stop a person who enters a police station and states that he wishes to confess to a crime, or a person who calls the police to offer a confession or any other statement he desires to make. Volunteered statements of any kind are not barred by the Fifth Amendment and their admissibility is not affected by our holding today.

To summarize, we hold that when an individual is taken into custody or otherwise deprived of his freedom by the authorities and is subjected to questioning, the privilege against self-incrimination is jeopardized. Procedural safeguards must be employed to protect the privilege, and unless other fully effective means are adopted to notify the person of his right of silence and to assure that the exercise of the right will be scrupulously honored, the following measures are required. He must be warned prior to any questioning that he has the right to remain silent, that anything he says can be used against him in a court of law, that he has the right to the presence of an attorney, and that if he cannot afford an attorney one will be appointed for him prior to any questioning if he so desires. Opportunity to exercise these rights must be afforded to him throughout the interrogation. After such warnings have been given, and such opportunity afforded him, the individual may knowingly and intelligently waive these rights and agree to answer questions or make a statement. But unless and until such warnings and waiver are demonstrated by the prosecution at trial, no evidence obtained as a result of interrogation can be used against him.

The *Miranda* opinion adds a fourth level to the broadening definition of "voluntary." Starting with (1) the patent involuntariness in *Brown, Ashcraft,* and *Leyra* (involving torture, prolonged questioning, and hypnosis, respectively), the Court eventually found (2) the subtle trick in *Spano* and (3) the threat of incommunicado detention in *Haynes* also unconstitutional. Finally, (4) *Miranda* establishes an "inherently involuntary" presumption, which will be removed if certain mitigating warnings are given. These warnings are the suspect's constitutional rights to be silent, not to incriminate himself, and to a lawyer (for free, if necessary). The right to a lawyer arises for the same reason that the warnings are necessary—the accusatory process has begun. The warnings will hopefully relieve the coercion inherent in that process, and the lawyer will hopefully safeguard rights which, without his aid, might be lost.

Justices Clark, Harlan, Stewart, and White dissented. They disagreed with the Court's legal and factual premises and conclusions. They did not believe that the Fifth Amendment's privilege against self-incrimination did or should extend as far as the majority thought. *Miranda* is a five to four decision—but its continuing vitality is uncertain. Justice Marshall has replaced Justice Clark and he is likely to support the *Miranda* holding. However, Chief Justice Warren Burger and Justice

Harry A. Blackmun have replaced Chief Justice Warren and Justice Fortas, respectively, and we shall have to wait to learn their views. Justice Harlan now follows *Miranda,* not because he has changed his mind, but because he considers himself bound by it. He may no longer consider himself bound, however, if his view musters a majority.

While *Miranda* reigns, there are questions it continues to present. An immediate one is whether the *Miranda* warnings are constitutionally required. The Court said that they were required "unless other fully effective means are derived to inform accused persons of their right of silence and to assure a continuous opportunity to exercise it." Would any other means be as "fully effective," short of giving every suspect a chance to speak to an attorney prior to questioning?

Warnings are necessary to remove the inherent coerciveness of *custodial* interrogation, and, without them, all statements will be presumed involuntary. "Custody," then, refers to those situations where an element of inherent coercion is present. Three examples will clarify this.

In *Mathis* v. *United States,* 391 U.S. 1 (1968), an Internal Revenue Agent questioned Mathis about prior tax returns while he was in jail for a state crime. The agent did not give the *Miranda* warnings and Mathis made certain admissions. A majority of the Court said the *Miranda* warnings were necessary because the questioning had occurred in a coercive situation. The three dissenters did not believe *Miranda*-type coercion was present.

Miranda rested not on the mere fact of physical restriction but on a conclusion that coercion—pressure to answer questions—usually flows from a certain type of custody, police station interrogation of someone charged with or suspected of a crime. Although [Mathis] was confined, he was at the time of interrogation in familiar surroundings. . . . The rationale of *Miranda* has no relevance to inquiries conducted outside the allegedly hostile and forbidding atmosphere surrounding police station interrogation of a criminal suspect.

Mathis and *Orozco* v. *Texas,* 394 U.S. 324 (1969), clearly indicate that, despite the arguments of the *Mathis* dissent, the test is coercion under any factual situation; the questioning need not occur in a stationhouse. In *Orozco,* the defendant shot a man after a quarrel that began when the victim accosted the defendant's female companion. The victim apparently hit the defendant in the face and called him "Mexican Grease." After the shooting, the defendant went to his boardinghouse. He was awakened at 4:00 A.M. when four policemen entered his bedroom and started questioning him. The defendant made certain statements leading to his conviction. He was not given the *Miranda* warnings. The State argued that the warnings were not required because the defendant was in familiar surroundings. The Court acknowledged that compulsion to speak is greatest in the police station, but held that the warnings must be given whenever, and apparently wherever, a suspect is in custody or has his freedom of action limited. The defendant was under arrest as soon as the police learned his identity and his freedom of action was clearly limited.

Justice Harlan concurred, believing himself bound by *Miranda* and *Mathis;* Justices White and Stewart dissented.

The police need not give the *Miranda* warnings to a person if he is not in custody or under any limitation on his freedom of action. This is true even though the police have probable cause to make an arrest, but choose not to. Since there is no coercion or coercive situation, warnings are not required. For example, a lower federal court determined that the confession in *Allen* v. *United States,* 390 F.2d 476 (1968), was admissible even though the warnings were absent. In *Allen,* a policeman in the District of Columbia spotted a car driving without headlights at night and he stopped it. Inside was the driver (Allen) and a badly beaten man (Jeffries). The officer asked Jeffries who had beaten him. Jeffries mumbled something unintelligible and pointed to Allen. The officer asked Allen if he had beaten Jeffries and Allen said he had. The Court said this confession was properly admitted against Allen.

We think the relative routineness of an inquiry is a material indicator that the police are still in a state of investigation. The police talk to too many people in the course of a day to make warnings compulsory every time they inquire into a situation. Such a requirement would hamper and perhaps demean routine police investigation. Indeed excessive admonitions are likely to make cooperative and law-abiding citizens anxious and fearful out of proportion to the need for admonitions in advising prime suspects of their rights.[5]

The police response to *Miranda* has not been exuberant. The Federal Bureau of Investigation, which apparently views the case as requiring it to get suspects to waive their rights, asks them to sign the following form before questioning begins.

INTERROGATION: ADVICE OF RIGHTS

Your Rights

Before we ask you any question, you must understand your rights. You have the right to remain silent.

Anything you say can be used against you in court.

You have the right to talk to a lawyer for advice before we ask you any questions and to have him with you during questioning.

If you cannot afford a lawyer, one will be appointed for you before any questioning if you wish.

If you decide to answer questions now without a lawyer present, you will still have the right to stop answering at anytime. You also have the right to stop answering at any time until you talk to a lawyer.

[5] Recall *Terry* v. *Ohio* in Chapter 4. Is it fair to say, in light of *Allen,* that the police need not give *Miranda* warnings prior to a *Terry*-type stop and search?

Waiver of Rights

I have read this statement of my rights and I understand what my rights are. I am willing to make a statement and answer questions. I do not want a lawyer at this time. I understand and know what I am doing. No promises or threats have been made to me and no pressure or coercion of any kind has been used against me.

Signed _____

Witness: _____
Witness: _____
Time: _____

Three law review articles have reported the post-*Miranda* practices of local police in New Haven, Pittsburg, and Washington, D.C.[6] These articles conclude that the police frequently fail to give the warnings, or do not give them in full. The New Haven study reported that the police sometimes hedged in stating the warnings, telling the suspect, for example, "you don't have to talk but . . ." When the warnings are given, suspects generally fail to appreciate them or really grasp their rights. In other words, the warnings do not significantly reduce the coercion inherent in the interrogation process.

This conclusion is also supported in a subsequent article in the Yale Law Journal.[7] Twenty–one faculty members and students at Yale turned in their draft cards as part of an antiwar protest. The FBI eventually questioned these twenty–one people in their own homes and offices. Some, but not all, received warnings at the outset. The others were either never warned, or were warned only after they had answered a question about the

[6] "Interrogations in New Haven: The Impact of Miranda," 76 *Yale Law Journal* 1519 (1967); Seeburger and Wettick, "Miranda in Pittsburgh—A Statistical Study," 29 *University of Pittsburgh Law Review* 1 (1967); Medalie, Leitz & Alexander, "Custodial Police Interrogation in Our Nation's Capitol: The Attempt to Implement Miranda," 66 *Michigan Law Review* 1347 (1968).

[7] Griffiths & Ayres, "A Postscript to the Miranda Project: Interrogation of Draft Protesters," 77 *Yale Law Journal* 300 (1967).

location of their draft cards—the very crime under investigation! Since the questioning occurred while the suspects were not in custody or in another coercive situation, it is arguable that *Miranda* did not apply. The startling conclusion of the article, however, is that even when the warnings were given, articulate, educated persons in friendly surroundings did not completely appreciate their rights, but felt *obligated* to talk. Silence was seen as rude. Middle-class values required a response. The agents were in complete control of the conversations and the suspects found it difficult to effectively terminate them.

Congressional Reaction

Title II of the Omnibus Crime Control and Safe Streets Act of 1968[8] represents the Congressional reaction to *Miranda* and *Escobedo.* The law permits the trial judge to consider the totality of the surrounding circumstances in making a determination of the voluntariness of a confession. No one factor, such as the suspect's knowledge of his rights, would be controlling. The effect is a return to *Haynes* v. *Washington,* or perhaps even *Spano* v. *New York.* The relevant section states:

The trial judge in determining the issue of voluntariness shall take into consideration all the circumstances surrounding the giving of the confession, including (1) the time elapsing between arrest and arraignment of the defendant making the confession, if it was made after arrest and before arraignment, (2) whether such defendant knew the nature of the offense with which he was charged or of which he was suspected at the time of making the confession, (3) whether or not such defendant was advised or knew that he was not required to make any statement and that any such statement could be used against him, (4) whether or not such de-

---

[8] This is the same law that contained the provisions for wiretapping and eavesdropping and the provision overruling the McNabb-Mallory line of cases.

fendant had been advised prior to questioning of his right to the assistance of counsel; and (5) whether or not such defendant was without the assistance of counsel when questioned and when giving such confession.

The presence or absence of any of the above-mentioned factors to be taken into consideration by the judge need not be conclusive on the issue of voluntariness of the confession.

The Court is resourceful. It might determine that despite the apparent conflict between *Miranda* and the statute they are really in accord. To reach that result, the Court will either have to dilute the case or "read in" to the statute. For example, the Court might determine that the words "need not" in the final sentence do not apply to factors (3) and (4), that the presence of those factors *is* conclusive on the issue of voluntariness.[9] Or the Court might face the problem directly and hold that *Miranda,* since it is based on the Constitution, prevails over a conflicting statute. A plain reading of the law leads to the inevitable conclusion that Congress wanted to overrule the case. Whether the Court will choose to read plainly is a question it will someday have to answer.[10]

Eyewitness Identification

The *Escobedo-Miranda* "revolution" has affected a collateral area that has long been ignored: eyewitness identification. Juries are immensely impressed when the victim of or a witness

[9] For a discussion of the various ways in which the Court can handle this problem see the Comment on title II in 82 *Harvard Law Review* 1392 (1969).

[10] That day may come very soon. The Justice Department plans to offer into evidence confessions which, inadvertently, were not preceded by *Miranda* warnings but which the Department believes satisfy the requirements of title II. The Department will argue that the *Miranda* case merely suggests one possible way to assure voluntary confessions, but that Congress is not foreclosed from substituting a more flexible alternative *The New York Times,* July 28, 1969, p. 1, col. 4.

to a crime points his finger at the defendant in court and states unequivocally: "Yes, that's the man." Ironically, this powerful testimony is often unreliable and wrong. Contributing to this unreliability is the manner in which lineups and other identification procedures are conducted. Frequently a witness who, in court, identifies the defendant as the guilty one recalls not the crime itself, but the intervening lineup or identification proceeding. The witness points to the man he remembers choosing at the lineup, not the person he may remember at the scene of the crime. To the witness they are the same person because he honestly believes he correctly identified the guilty man at the lineup. But because lineups are frequently, though not intentionally, "set up" to increase the likelihood that the wrong man might be identified, there is a real chance that the witness is wrong.[11]

Courts have begun to realize this and during the past few years in-court identification has not been allowed if an intervening lineup or other procedure was "so unnecessarily suggestive and conducive to irreparable mistaken identification" as to equal a denial of due process of law.[12] The facts in *Foster* v. *California,* 394 U.S. 440 (1969), illustrate this kind of due process denial.

[T]his case presents a compelling example of unfair lineup procedures. In the first lineup arranged by the police, petitioner stood out from the other two men by the contrast of his height and by the fact that he was wearing a leather jacket similar to that worn by the robber. . . . When this did not lead to positive identification, the police permitted a one-to-one confrontation between petitioner and the witness. This Court pointed out in *Stovall* that "[t]he practice of showing suspects singly to persons for the purpose of identification, and not as part of a lineup, has been widely

[11] P. Wall, *Eye-Witness Identification in Criminal Cases* (Springfield, Ill.: Charles C Thomas, 1965) is an excellent discussion with many disturbing examples. See also, *The New York Post*, April 2, 1970, p. 49 for an example of mistaken identity that nearly sent a man to prison.
[12] The language is from *Stovall* v. *Denno*, 388 U.S. 293 (1967).

condemned." . . . Even after this witness' identification of petitioner was tentative. So some days later another lineup was arranged. Petitioner was the only person in this lineup who had also
participated in the first lineup. . . . This finally produced a definite
identification.

The suggestive elements in this identification procedure made it
all but inevitable that [the witness] would identify petitioner
whether or not he was in fact "the man." In effect, the police
repeatedly said to the witness, "*This* is the man." . . . This procedure so undermined the reliability of the eyewitness identification
as to violate due process.[13]

The five to four split in *Foster* indicates the difficulty the
courts will necessarily have in determining whether the circumstances surrounding a particular identification were, in fact, so
conducive to being mistaken as to violate due process. In some
cases, convictions will be reversed, though proper precautions
would have avoided that result. In other cases, the errors,
though unfairly prejudicial, will not rise to constitutional mag-
nitude. This is an area in which an ounce of prevention can do
a lot. Accordingly, the Supreme Court has attempted to assure
fairness at lineups by declaring them to be a "critical" stage of
the criminal process and, therefore, counsel must be provided.
The case is *United States* v. *Wade,* 388 U.S. 218 (1967) and
the Court said:

[T]he confrontation compelled by the State between the accused
and the victim or witnesses to a crime to elicit identification evidence is peculiarly riddled with innumerable dangers and variable
factors which might seriously, even crucially, derogate from a fair
trial. The vagaries of eyewitness identification are well-known; the
annals of criminal law are rife with instances of mistaken identification. . . . A major factor contributing to the high incidence of
miscarriage of justice from mistaken identification has been the
degree of suggestion inherent in the manner in which the prosecu-

[13] In Chapter 3 we noted that certain procedures may violate due
process without violating any of the particular guarantees in the Bill of
Rights. This is one of them.

tion presents the suspect to witnesses for pretrial identification. A commentator has observed that "[t]he influence of improper suggestion upon identifying witnesses probably accounts for more miscarriages of justice than any other single factor—perhaps it is responsible for more such errors than all other factors combined." [Wall, *Eye-Witness Identification in Criminal Cases*, p. 26.] Suggestion can be created intentionally or unintentionally in many subtle ways. And the dangers for the suspect are particularly grave when the witness' opportunity for observation was insubstantial, and thus his susceptibility to suggestion the greatest.

Moreover, "[i]t is a matter of common experience that, once a witness has picked out the accused at the lineup, he is not likely to go back on his word later on, so that in practice the issue of identity may (in the absence of other relevant evidence) for all practical purposes be determined there and then, before the trial." . . .

In short, the accused's inability effectively to reconstruct at trial any unfairness that occurred at the lineup may deprive him of his only opportunity meaningfully to attack the credibility of the witness' courtroom identification. . . .

Thus, in the present context, where so many variables and pitfalls exist, the first line of defense must be the prevention of unfairness and the lessening of the hazards of eyewitness identification at the lineup itself. The trial which might determine the accused's fate may well not be that in the courtroom but that at the pretrial confrontation, with the state aligned against the accused, the witness the sole jury, and the accused unprotected against the overreaching, intentional or unintentional, and with little or no effective appeal from the judgment there rendered by the witness—"that's the man." . . .

Thus both Wade and his counsel should have been notified of the impending lineup, and counsel's presence should have been a requisite to conduct of the lineup, absent an "intelligent waiver."

If the *Wade* requirement is not followed, the in-court identification may still be allowed if the state can show it will not be tainted by the illegal lineup. In other words, where the state conducts a lineup or pretrial identification without counsel, and the identification does not otherwise violate due process, in-court identification will be permitted if the witness is basing his identification on his memory of the crime rather than his memory of the illegal pretrial procedure. *Gilbert* v. *California,* 388 U.S. 263 (1967).

The Court's concern for pretrial identification is balanced by the realization that visual identification is essential to the effective investigation of crime. Thus, in *Simmons* v. *United States,* 390 U.S. 377 (1968), the Court upheld in-court identification of Simmons by bank employees even though the employees had been shown pictures of possible suspects the day after the bank robbery. Simmons' photograph was among the pictures shown. The FBI procedure in the particular case, said the Court, was not "so impermissibly suggestive as to give rise to a very substantial likelihood of irreparable misidentification." In addition, the circumstances were compelling. The bank had been robbed, and the robbers were free. Swift action was essential.

Similarly, in *Stovall* v. *Denno,* the police displayed a single suspect to a seriously wounded woman. The woman could not go to the police station and the length of time she might live was uncertain. Since to postpone identification in this case meant the possibility of losing all chance of it, the police action was held constitutional.

What is the extent of the right to counsel at lineups? *Wade* guarantees counsel *at* the lineup, but counsel is also needed before and after the lineup, when witnesses are briefed and debriefed. Improper procedures during these periods can also result in misidentification. For example, after a recent lineup an FBI agent asked a witness: "All right, now, is it one, two, three, four, or five?" There was no suggestion that it might have been none of these.

Finally, in this area too, Congress has spoken through the Omnibus Crime Control Bill. Assuming the following provision could constitutionally overrule the Supreme Court's decisions, does it in fact do so?

The testimony of a witness that he saw the accused commit or participate in the commission of the crime for which the accused is being tried shall be admissible in evidence in a criminal prosecution in any [federal] trial court. . . .

8

A NOTE ON
JUVENILE
JUSTICE

The rules we have been discussing were developed in the context of adult criminal trials. In that context, the courts try to
balance the individual's rights to privacy and a fair trial with
the people's interest in preventing and solving crimes.[1] When
antisocial conduct is committed by a juvenile, however, Congress
and the state legislatures have introduced another consideration:
The assumption is that the juvenile offender, more than his adult
counterpart, is receptive to treatment and correction, that he is
not "hardened," and that he should be treated, when possible,
outside the criminal process. As a result, juvenile justice systems
are comparatively informal and are supposed to include the
services of trained professionals, including psychologists and
social workers.

Informality and a broad social orientation represent an important addition to the traditionally narrow ("we-they") criminal justice system, but these factors are potentially in conflict
with the suspect's parallel interest in due process. To what extent
can the state compromise constitutional rights on the ground

[1] An "individual v. state" perspective is not universally accepted as the
inevitable structure for all criminal justice systems. See Griffiths, "Ideology
in Criminal Procedures," *or* "A Third Model of the Criminal Process,"
79 *Yale Law Journal* 359 (1970).

that it has substituted the traditional criminal process with an enlightened one, to which it might not even attach the label "criminal?"

This is not a mere academic question. It is potentially present in every juvenile arrest and trial.[2] And there are many—persons under eighteen years of age committed 37 percent of the crimes reported and solved in the United States in 1969 based on reports from 3,814 cities with a total population of 98,444,000.[3] For certain serious offenses, the relevant percentages are:

Murder and non-negligent manslaughter	6.1 percent (6,515 total clearances)
Negligent manslaughter	5.0 percent (3,184)
Forcible rape	14.2 percent (10,011)
Robbery	23.3 percent (41,302)
Aggravated assault	10.6 percent (101,578)
Burglary	40.3 percent (196,916)
Larceny—no limit	42.3 percent (403,270)
Larceny over $50	29.4 percent (92,655)
Auto theft	48.0 percent (92,239)

The number of juveniles arrested (whether or not their guilt is ultimately determined) is also relevant to the scope of this problem. Thus, reports from law enforcement agencies serving 143,815,000 people indicate that persons under fifteen accounted for 9.7 percent of all arrests in 1969 and 21.8 percent of arrests for the serious felonies listed in the above chart.

[2] Nor is it limited to the juvenile criminal process, but it is relevant whenever the state seeks to exchange an individual's constitutional rights for some special benefit.

[3] FBI Crime Reports (1969). The total of crimes solved was 855,015.

When the age is raised to eighteen, the respective percentages are 25.6 and 47.7, and persons under twenty-one accounted for 38.9 percent of all arrests and 64.0 percent of arrests for the listed felonies. The FBI's statistics are subject to error because they reflect the records only of those agencies reporting and because not all crime is reported to the authorities. Nevertheless, the inescapable conclusion is that persons under twenty-one and even persons under eighteen are responsible for a large amount of crime—and particularly serious crime.[4]

One half of the persons under eighteen who are arrested eventually appear in court. Virtually all of those appear in a juvenile court, a tribunal supposedly better equipped to handle problems associated with young offenders. What are the rights of a suspect in a juvenile court? How do they differ from the rights of adult offenders in traditional tribunals? To what extent do the juvenile court's rehabilitative goals legally allow it to deny certain of the criminal court's constitutional safeguards? These questions received surprisingly little attention from the Supreme Court until 1967 and the landmark decision of *In re Gault,* 387 U.S. 1 (1967).

Gerald Gault and a friend were taken into custody after a woman neighbor (Mrs. Cook) complained about a lewd telephone call. Gerald was picked up while his parents were at work; no message was left for them. Gerald's mother learned where he was only after inquiry, and she was then told by the superintendent of the detention center (Officer Flagg) "why Jerry was there" and that a hearing would be held the next day, June 9, in the juvenile court. The remaining facts follow from the Court's opinion:

Officer Flagg filed a petition with the Court on the hearing day, June 9, 1964. It was not served on the Gaults. Indeed, none of them saw this petition until the habeas corpus hearing on August

---

[4] The various states have different age limits, after which a suspect may no longer be referred to a juvenile court. The limit is generally lower than twenty-one.

17, 1964. The petition was entirely formal. It made no reference to any factual basis for the judicial action which it initiated. It recited only that "said minor is under the age of eighteen years and in need of the protection of this Honorable Court [and that] said minor is a delinquent minor." It prayed for a hearing and an order regarding "the care and custody of said minor." Officer Flagg executed a formal affidavit in support of the petition.

On June 9, Gerald, his mother, his older brother, and Probation Officers Flagg and Henderson appeared before the Juvenile Judge in chambers. Gerald's father was not there. He was at work out of the city. Mrs. Cook, the complainant, was not there. No one was sworn at this hearing. No transcript or recording was made. No memorandum or record of the substance of the proceedings was prepared. Our information about the proceedings and the subsequent hearing on June 15, derives entirely from the testimony of the Juvenile Court Judge, Mr. and Mrs. Gault and Officer Flagg at the habeas corpus proceeding conducted two months later. From this, it appears that at the July 9 hearing Gerald was questioned by the judge about the telephone call. There was conflict as to what he said. His mother recalled that Gerald said he only dialed Mrs. Cook's number and handed the telephone to his friend, Ronald. Officer Flagg recalled that Gerald had admitted making the lewd remarks. Judge McGhee testified that Gerald "admitted making one of these [lewd] statements." At the conclusion of the hearing, the judge said he would "think about it." Gerald was taken back to the Detention Home. He was not sent to his own home with his parents. On June 11 or 12, after having been detained since June 8, Gerald was released and driven home. There is no explanation in the record as to why he was kept in the Detention Home or why he was released. At 5 P.M. on the day of Gerald's release, Mrs. Gault received a note signed by Officer Flagg. It was on plain paper, not letterhead. Its entire text was as follows:

"Mrs. Gault:
"Judge McGHEE has set Monday June 15, 1964 at 11:00 A.M. as the date and time for further Hearings on Gerald's delinquency

[s] Flagg"

At the appointed time on Monday, June 15, Gerald, his father and mother, Ronald Lewis and his father, and Officers Flagg and

Henderson were present before Judge McGhee. Witnesses at the habeas corpus proceeding differed in their recollections of Gerald's testimony at the June 15 hearing. Mr. and Mrs. Gault recalled that Gerald again testified that he had only dialed the number and that the other boy had made the remarks. Officer Flagg agreed that at this hearing Gerald did not admit making the lewd remarks. But Judge McGhee recalled that "there was some admission again of some of the lewd statements. He—he didn't admit any of the more serious lewd statements." Again, the complainant, Mrs. Cook, was not present. Mrs. Gault asked that Mrs. Cook be present "so she could see which boy had done the talking, the dirty talking over the phone." The Juvenile Judge said "she didn't have to be present at that hearing." The judge did not speak to Mrs. Cook or communicate with her at any time. Probation Officer Flagg had talked to her once—over the telephone on June 9.

At this June 15 hearing a "referral report" made by the probation officers was filed with the court, although not disclosed to Gerald or his parents. This listed the charge as "Lewd Phone Calls." At the conclusion of the hearing, the judge committed Gerald as a juvenile delinquent to the State Industrial School, "for the period of his minority [that is, until twenty-one], unless sooner discharged by due process of law." An order to that effect was entered. It recites that "after a full hearing and due deliberation the Court finds that said minor is a delinquent child, and that said minor is of the age of fifteen years."

The Arizona courts denied Gerald habeas corpus relief, and he sought review in the United States Supreme Court. There, his lawyers argued that the Arizona procedure denied Gerald Fourteenth Amendment due process because it did not afford him the following fundamental rights:

1. the right to adequate notice of the charges against him;
2. the right to counsel;
3. the right to confront and cross-examine witnesses against him (i.e., Mrs. Cook);
4. the privilege against self-incrimination;
5. the right to a transcript of the proceedings; and
6. the right to an appeal from a determination of guilt.

The Supreme Court only ruled on the first four of these claims,

reserving decision on the last two. Other constitutional guarantees of adult offenders, not raised in *Gault,* are also left for
future decision.

Before the Court could decide whether the Due Process
Clause required the application of the first four rights just mentioned to juvenile criminal (or delinquency) proceedings, it had
to decide whether the Due Process Clause itself applied to such
proceedings. In holding that it did apply, the Court stressed
that its decision was limited to the adjudicatory, or fact-finding,
stage of those proceedings. This is the stage in which the facts
are decided and a determination of guilt or innocence made.
"We are not here concerned," said the Court, "with the procedures or constitutional rights applicable to the pre-judicial
stages of the juvenile process, nor do we direct our attention
to the post-adjudicative or dispositional process."

This limitation is understandable. As we noted earlier, the
juvenile court movement was accompanied by a belief that
juvenile offenders should be treated differently from adult
offenders. The reformists believed that the state should be free
to deal with a juvenile delinquent in a variety of ways, depending on the facts of the particular case and the problems of the
particular child. For example, there should be a procedure by
which a determination of guilt or innocence could be completely
avoided if that, under all the circumstances, were the best thing
to do. Accordingly, the *Gault* Court expressly disavowed any
interference with procedures at this "pre-judicial" stage of the
juvenile process.

On the other hand, once a determination of guilt has already
been made, the juvenile court, and the agencies that service it,
must be free to apply the remedy best-suited to the problems of
the particular child. Since the goal is rehabilitation, success will
require flexibility and freedom from "technical" legal restraints.
Thus, the *Gault* Court also disavowed interference with this
"post-adjudicative or dispositional process."

When the guilt-determination stage is involved, however, the need for flexibility is less apparent and the need for traditional constitutional guarantees more so. For at this stage, the question is: what are the facts? And the answer will require a reconstruction of past events. At adult hearings, constitutional procedural safeguards are intended to assure that such a reconstruction is made accurately. Since the adjudicatory stages of the adult and juvenile processes are alike, the guarantees that are intended to produce the truth at the first stage should apply at the second.

But this explanation only accounts for the court's willingness to apply certain of the due process safeguards to the adjudicatory stage of the juvenile process. At least one of the safeguards applied in *Gault,* the privilege against self-incrimination, is not primarily intended to assure an accurate reconstruction of past events, but rather serves to protect the dignity of the individual. The Court recognized this when it said:

> The privilege against self-incrimination is, of course, related to the question of the safeguards necessary to assure that admissions or confessions are reasonably trustworthy, that they are not the mere fruits of fear or coercion, but are reliable expressions of the truth. The roots of the privilege are, however, far deeper. They tap the basic stream of religious and political principle because the privilege reflects the limits of the individual's attornment to the state and—in a philosophical sense—insists upon the equality of the individual and the state. In other words, the privilege has a broader and deeper thrust than the rule which prevents the use of confessions which are the product of coercion because coercion is thought to carry with it the danger of unreliability. One of its purposes is to prevent the State, whether by force or by psychological domination, from overcoming the mind and will of the person under investigation and depriving him of the freedom to decide whether to assist the state in securing his conviction.

Once it held that the Due Process Clause applied to the adjudicatory stage of the juvenile process, the Court had to consider what specific requirements of that Clause, if any, were violated on the facts before it. It held that four of the rights urged by Gerald Gault—to notice of the charges, to counsel, to confrontation and cross-examination of witnesses, and against self-incrimination—were improperly denied him. It is noteworthy that the two rights on which the Court did not reach a decision—to a transcript of the hearing and to appeal—have not yet been constitutionally required in adult criminal proceedings either.

In addition to the express limitation of *Gault* to the adjudicatory stage of the juvenile process, the decision is conceivably subject to another limitation. Gerald Gault was charged with a crime that would also have been a crime if committed by an adult. There are many offenses, however, which, by definition can be committed only by juveniles (for example, truancy, running away, and being incorrigible). Are the *Gault* guarantees present when these offenses are charged? Probably they are, at least where commitment to an institution is a possible consequence of conviction. The *Gault* Court did not emphasize whether Gerald's offense would also be a crime if committed by an adult; on the contrary, it stressed that Gerald, as a result of his conviction, could be (and actually was) committed to a state institution until he was twenty-one, a period of six years. It was the possibility of commitment that triggered the criminal guarantees of the Constitution.

Justice Black concurred and Justice Harlan concurred in part. True to their respective views, Justice Black believed that all of the rights in the first eight amendments applied in the juvenile court, and Justice Harlan contended that only those rights necessary for "fundamental fairness" were constitutionally compelled. Justice Harlan believed fundamental fairness required that the defendant have notice of the charges against him and the assistance of appointed or retained counsel. And, although the Court did not reach the issue, Justice Harlan said that juvenile defendants should have a right to a transcript of their hearings. Justice White concurred in part and Justice Stewart dissented.

Another problem in the juvenile area is the standard of proof necessary for conviction. Proof beyond a reasonable doubt is required at adult criminal trials, but most states, perhaps because juvenile proceedings were not considered criminal, used a lesser standard in juvenile matters. The Court held this procedure impermissible in *In re Winship,* 397 U.S. 358 (1970). Proof beyond a reasonable doubt is a constitutional requirement for adults and juveniles both.

The lesson of *Gault* is that the state's willingness, in the interests of rehabilitation, to be flexible and informal when a juvenile is charged with antisocial conduct, may, at some point, clash with the traditional constitutional guarantees.

In such a case, the courts may choose the benefit to be derived from informality or it may, as in *Gault,* hold that the particular constitutional rule at issue is paramount. Or a court may attempt to salvage the best of both approaches. Because the juvenile court movement is supposedly an enlightened one that works in the child's best interests, the courts will be reluctant to frustrate its goals with rigid constitutional requirements. But the extent to which the courts will permit the State to compromise constitutional guarantees for the avowed goal of saving the child will depend on just how seriously the State pursues that goal. If, for example, the young offender is treated no differently from an adult, there is no reason why the courts should permit the state to deny him any rights assured to adults. On the other hand, if the state has well-staffed correctional facilities or probation services for juvenile offenders, the courts will be less likely to intervene. This is especially true for the two stages of the juvenile process—the pre-judicial and the dispositional —which *Gault* did not reach, for it is at these stages that an enlightened juvenile system can have its most productive effect.

Unfortunately, the evidence is that correctional facilities for juveniles are at best medieval, as the following extensive excerpts from Congressman Bertram Podell's testimony indicate:[5]

[5] Testimony of Hon. Bertram L. Podell before the United States Senate Subcommittee to investigate juvenile delinquency (July 7, 1969).

While a member of the New York State Legislature, I served as Chairman of the Joint Legislative Committee on Penal Institutions. During my tenure, I visited and inspected almost every penal institution dealing with juveniles in New York State. Senator, those sights, sounds and smells will haunt my memories for the rest of my life.

Bright spots exist. Dedicated people labor. A few are saved. But our facilities, from detention centers to youth facilities and remand centers are colleges of crime which are utter failures as far as changing future lives of inmates. A few are modern day devil's islands, comparable to the worst horrors of the last century. As an American and a legislator, I am ashamed.

Speaking from personal experience and observation, we are taking unnumbered thousands of juvenile offenders at a crucial point in their lives and turning them into hardened, professional criminals. In every facility charged with overseeing and rehabilitating young offenders, they are professionally neglected and abused, thrown into hellholes in which they receive post graduate criminal education. Ignored and brutalized, their lives are wrenched asunder by those who are charged with the duty of watching them. I witnessed the destruction of part of tomorrow's generation in institution after institution.

From top to bottom, the system juvenile offenders are thrown into is rife with incompetents, inadequate facilities and professional brutality. If it is not halted forthwith, we shall destroy the very essence of our society. The overwhelming majority of these young people return to society worse off than when they entered the institution, prepared to perpetrate worse atrocities upon themselves and society. It is the most disgusting national disgrace I have ever witnessed. . . .

We have not even begun to make a dent in the unbelievably sordid warping of this unique concept. I cannot emphasize too strongly how necessary reform is in this area. As it operates today, it makes a terrible reality out of the claimed double standard of justice for the rich and laws for the poor.

At the Brooklyn Adolescent Center, I found a warden with no regard for the 1,100-odd boys in his care. Crowded like cattle in cars, these youngsters had nothing to do but sit and brood all day long. Perversion was rampant. Brutality was obvious. There is a gym which is unused because the warden uses it to practice his golf game. He stated to me personally that basketballs would scuff that shiny floor. His utter lack of concern was so utterly revolting as to stay vivid in my memory to this moment.

Mattresses are nonexistent. Springs with sheets thrown over them are all that is provided for sleeping purposes. Towels are not issued. They must be brought. The same is true of toothbrushes. In truth, anyone brought to this center is guilty before trial. The only prevailing crime committed by these youngsters is poverty. Unable to raise bail—ignored by society—they fester massively in an environment which would make a criminal out of a saint. A true breeding ground for our penitentiaries.

This is a common picture of a situation prevailing in most, if not all, of the juvenile detention centers of New York State, which is supposed to set a standard for our nation.

In the midst of terrible crowding in these facilities, homosexuality and every other imaginable deviation is rampant. Gang rapes are common. Almost all these institutions serve as recruiting centers for groups such as the Black Muslims. Hardened older criminals organize gangs and dominate the scenes.

Upstate New York facilities are almost always located 50 to 100 miles away from the homes of these youngsters. Poor parents find it almost impossible to reach them for regular visiting purposes.

Youth centers are just as uniformly bad, if not worse than detention centers. Youth House in New York City comes immediately to mind. Children in such institutions are sent there from age seven. Not only those who are delinquents, but unwanted children as well. Nine, ten and eleven-year-olds are herded together with older homosexuals, muggers and psychopaths in a grotesque tangle. Brutal guards who practice homosexuality are too often encountered.

In upstate reformatories, a girl as young as fourteen may be and is too often thrown in with a hardened, eighteen-year-old prostitute. The younger girl could be there because of parental commitment as a runaway. By the time she is finally released, she has learned the rudiments of a profitable trade, courtesy of the State.

Why is there such an institution as Youth House? It is a collecting point for our unwanted, left there for days, weeks and longer. The three major religions maintain their own shelters or facilities. Remaining children who cannot get into charity-sponsored homes are relegated to Youth House.

I remember talking to a girl who had had a baby in Youth House the night before she appeared in court. She had cut the umbilical cord with her teeth, and hid the child under her dress in court.

There are reformatories and institutions in New York State which provide excellent programs in conservation camps. A model inmate is allowed into them on an honor system. There he learns a trade, such as conservation, forestry, lumbering or farming. The program is run by the New York State Department of Correction in conjunction with the New York State Department of Conservation. Once a boy is released, however, the Department of Conservation will not hire him because he possesses a prison record.

What good does it do to rehabilitate as the only real door to profitable upgrading employment is slammed shut in the faces of those who try to change? Their path must invariably return to the gates of our prisons.

Medical facilities are a farce, as is medical treatment. Staffs are composed of nurses only, who give aspirin and take temperatures. Medical help is only available at hospitals. Check-in procedures rarely include physical checkups. Several institutions do not give them at all. Uncooperative medical aid is common, complete with beatings. Girls' facilities do not offer proper prenatal or childbirth care. Inmates must bring their own clothing all too often, cleaning it themselves. Offenders picked up and awaiting trial possess only what is on their backs. Issued clothing is almost always old and torn. Towels, soap and personal supplies are not issued in some places. If an inmate has not had all his money stolen, he may purchase them. In one case, towels issued were made from torn sheets. Sometimes they are issued for one shower weekly only. Hands are washed without benefit of soap.

No regular Chaplain is available. When he does come, he has only a few moments with each inmate, depriving them of a potential source of rehabilitation.

Letters are often limited to two pages or twenty lines because the censor could not handle a greater volume. These were limited to one or two weekly, depending upon the institution.

In some institutions, shower and cleaning restrictions were severe. A shower and shave once or twice weekly was a common rule; seldom allowed daily. The stench must be experienced to be believed. Often toilet facilities and cleansing amenities were placed cheek by jowl. An institution in Monroe County dumped human wastes from hand carried slop buckets in to an open pit near showers, covering them with lye.

Guards are in short supply, often poorly trained. Some are professional sadists who don't even know what the word rehabilitation means. Examples of physical abuse are commonplace.

Psychological and psychiatric personnel are limited in numbers and available facilities. This potentially fruitful area of rehabilitation is a disaster area today.

Purposeful work activities are minimal. Vocational education or work is almost nowhere in evidence. Only a few of the best institutions possess proper equipment of this sort. A massive proportion of inmates spend their days in idleness, relieved only by graduate courses in crime. Cell facilities are often badly substandard. Erie County Penitentiary has no lights in its cells, eliminating useful reading.

Many buildings are visibly crumbling, complete with leaking roofs, cracked walls and sagging floors. Old buildings proliferate, having been built for other than detention purposes. Punishment is a scandal. Internal discipline is brutal, inhumane and animalistic, often far exceeding what is proper for an offense. One person received twenty days in solitary on bread and water for writing a letter to a newspaper.

Often those juveniles confined merely because they witnessed a crime fall victim to all these horrors. Greater injustice cannot be imagined. Thousands upon thousands of our young people emerge scarred for life by their shattering experiences.

Soaring recidivism rates are eloquent testimony to the truth of these claims . . . somewhere around one-fourth to one-third of all inmates. Brooklyn Youth Detention Center has a repeater rate of about 70 percent.

Many youngsters repose in these hellholes because of minor crimes. I found one who had broken a window and another who had committed the heinous crime of spitting in a subway.

Most juvenile facilities have massive turnovers. Most persons are on their way through, being processed for stays at other facilities or for trial. Adequate treatment for long term inmates is impossible. Short and long termers are not segregated, just as hardened youthful offenders are mixed in with civil cases.

In sum, juvenile penal institutions are tax-supported professional training camps for tomorrow's hardened criminals. New methods of committing old crimes are constantly taught. All this unacceptable activity is learned. We are not showing understanding of what is causing such behavior. Once in detention, juveniles are shown little, if any understanding, based on their backgrounds.

These young people are dependent, neglected, mentally retarded, mentally or emotionally disturbed and one-parent children. Often they are youngsters with school problems, from totally destructive city slum environments. Some are physically handicapped or outright delinquents.

Often children end up in detention centers because of minor crimes, such as skipping school, running away from often intolerable homes, fist fighting, drinking and stealing small quantities of candy, toys or clothing. Why are they then incarcerated in such environments where brutality replaces rehabilitation, and starkness replaces warmth and human understanding?

Often parents belong in prison rather than the children they have done their best to ruin. They undermine a child's self respect, giving him a warped idea or conception of himself. Physically brutal discipline is often encountered. Utter lack of supervision is also found. Divorce, separation, death and illness break their lives. Parental alcoholism, emotional imbalance, selfishness and instability do them severe harm. Neighborhood environments, gangs, lack of identification and emotional instability all go into the bag labeled causes of delinquency. These causes are hardly taken into consideration by those who are supposed not only to supervise juvenile incarceration, but rehabilitate such youngsters. Do we wonder then, at our repeater rate?

We are brutalizing youngsters in the name of rehabilitation. Ruining them in the name of penology. Mutilating them in the name of law and order.

So long as appalling conditions like these continue to exist, courts are less likely to be receptive to an argument that full constitutional guarantees should be denied in the best interests of the child. Indeed, certain language in *People* v. *Fuller,* 24 N.Y.2d 292 (1969), a case dealing with narcotics addiction, is relevant here. In *Fuller,* the state argued that a new program permitting it to commit certified narcotics addicts for treatment should be upheld even though the addict did not receive all the due process guarantees that the Constitution assures a criminal defendant. The New York Court of Appeals (the highest State court) agreed, but warned, in language equally applicable to the juvenile area, that the state must satisfactorily fulfill its half of the bargain and provide the promised treatment. Said the Court:

> If compulsory commitment turns out in fact to be a veneer for an extended jail term and is not a fully developed, comprehensive and effective scheme, it will have lost its claim to be a project devoted solely to curative ends. It will then take on the characteristics of normal jail sentence, with a side order of special help. The moment that the program begins to serve the traditional purposes of criminal punishment, such as deterrence, preventive detention, or retribution, then the extended denial of liberty is simply no different from a prison sentence . . . and the constitutional guarantees applicable to criminal proceedings will apply in full measure.

Earlier we mentioned a characteristic of most juvenile justice systems which could not constitutionally appear in an adult criminal system. A child may be committed for certain conduct, or for occupying a certain status, which could not be criminal if done, or occupied, by an adult. Examples include truancy, being wayward, being incorrigible, running away, and other "offenses."[6] Courts tolerate these "offenses" because they feel it is more important that a child in need of help receive it than that he be sacrificed to a nice constitutional theory. But if confinement is punitive and not rehabilitative, this toleration may disappear. In fact, a few courts have already ordered children released from institutions on proof that the state was not providing treatment when treatment was the state's justification for

---

[6] For example, the Arizona statute involved in *Gault* defines a "delinquent child" as:

a. A child who has violated a law of the state or an ordinance or regulation of a political subdivision thereof.

b. A child who, by reason of being incorrigible, wayward or habitually disobedient, is uncontrolled by his parent, guardian or custodian.

c. A child who is habitually truant from school or home.

d. A child who habitually so deports himself as to injure or endanger the morals or health of himself or others.

confinement in the first place.[7] The following excerpt from a recent law review article discusses the problem of "children's crimes":[8]

Under most juvenile laws, the fact that a child is "ungovernable" or beyond parental control brings him within the definition of delinquency—but what behavior is ungovernable? Whose values should be used to determine delinquency? Governability may well be a relative term, depending on whether or not there is a living father, a working mother, a permissive grandmother or a strict disciplinarian grandfather. As long as the standards remain vague and the police are aware that not only antisocial but mere asocial conduct may lead to an adjudication of delinquency, they end up subjectively deciding who is to be arrested and for what. With broad criteria, both the apprehension and adjudication of delinquency too often depend upon the child's socioeconomic background and upon the personal values of the particular police officer, the judge, or the court's social service staff. Indeed, the great variations in the number of reported delinquencies from community to community and from one social class to another may be attributed in part to the fact that in the more affluent settings many juvenile problems are handled by referral to other community agencies, without resort to police or court action. . . .

In the final analysis, the vague criteria for judicial intervention are due not so much to the lack of drafting skills as to the absence of a clear public consensus on the proper role of the juvenile court. Should the court serve as a tribunal of last resort or as the primary referral agency in the community? Is the court to deal with hard-core delinquents only, leaving preventive work to voluntary welfare agencies, or is it to do both? As one California legislative commission's report observed, the absence of a well-defined allocation of responsibilities and standards to guide juvenile court judges, welfare, probation, and law enforcement officials in their decisionmaking, may make juvenile dispositions depend more

[7] See, for example, *White* v. *Reid,* 125 F.Supp. 647 (1954); *In re Elmore,* 382 F.2d 125 (1967); *Creek* v. *Stone,* 379 F.2d 106 (1967). Vol. 57, no. 4 of the *Georgetown Law Journal* (March 1969) deals exclusively with the right to treatment.

[8] N. Kittrie, "Can the Right to Treatment Remedy the Ills of the Juvenile Process," 57 *Georgetown Law Journal* 848, 855–57 (1969) (footnotes omitted).

upon the community in which the juvenile is found than upon the intrinsic merits of the individual case. Such a result, as the commission pointed out, neither uniformly nor adequately protects basic legal rights.

The Supreme Court seemed ready to delve into this area when it noted probable jurisdiction in *Mattiello* v. *Connecticut,* 391 U.S. 963 (1968). A Connecticut court had found Frances Mattiello, an eighteen-year-old girl, guilty of "being in manifest danger of falling into vice" and of "lascivious carriage." Frances challenged her conviction on the first charge. The applicable statute said:

> Any unmarried female between the ages of sixteen and twenty-one years who is in manifest danger of falling into habits of vice, or who is leading a vicious life, or who has committed any crime may, upon the complaint of the prosecuting attorney of the circuit court, be brought before said court . . . and, upon conviction . . . may be committed, until she has arrived at the age of twenty-one years, to the custody of any institution . . . chartered . . . for the purpose of receiving and caring for females who have fallen into or are in danger of falling into vicious habits.

The state's appellate courts held the statute constitutional against a claim that "it purports to define a crime in language which is too vague and uncertain in its meaning to give adequate warning of the conduct proscribed or to guide courts in a fair administration of the law." The Connecticut court emphasized that the statute did not impose a criminal sanction. Rather its aims and purposes were "to preserve and increase the benefits to an orderly society deriving from the care, protection and welfare of the individuals who, because of lack of physical, mental, or moral resources or discipline, are especially in need of salutary aid and earnest concern on the part of the general public."[9] The implication is that the *quid pro quo* for the institutionalized juvenile is "salutary aid and earnest concern."

[9] 225 A.2d 507 (1966).

A court, however, should assure itself that aid and concern are, in fact, present before it permits the state to cite those reasons in justification of confinement. The idea that a state official can commit an eighteen-year-old girl to a jail-type institution for three years because he determines that the girl is falling into "habits of vice" or is leading a "vicious life" is repulsive. This power can only be justified, if at all, by a very real and very concerted effort on the part of the state to provide, unreservedly, the aid necessary to correct the very condition that the state contends authorizes confinement. Even then, courts should examine the particular conduct involved. Vague standards and moral self-righteousness may lead to an abuse of power which, masquerading as official benevolence, can go unnoticed or even applauded. *Gault* is hopefully the beginning of a long line of cases which will make the reality agree with the rhetoric. Unfortunately, the Supreme Court was not yet ready to examine this question in the case of Frances Mattiello and it dismissed her appeal.[10]

[10] A penetrating article analyzing *Gault,* written by two of the lawyers who took the case to the Supreme Court, is Dorsen and Rezneck, "In Re Gault and the Future of Juvenile Law," *Family Law Quarterly* (December 1967).

9

AVOIDING THE RULES:
OVERCRIMINALIZATION
AND POLICE LAWLESSNESS

This book is about criminal procedure—how laws are enforced. It is not about the substantive criminal law—what conduct is illegal. But "law enforcement" is a two-edged phrase; the manner of enforcement partially depends on the particular conduct the enforcer is expected to control. In this Chapter we will explore two ways in which the police can, and to some extent do, circumvent constitutional guarantees. First, overcriminalization—defining as criminal conduct that should be confronted, if at all, with a different societal response—and, second, police lawlessness, both undermine the effective assurance of constitutional criminal rights.

Overcriminalization

The plain sense that the criminal law is a highly specialized tool of social control, useful for certain purposes but not for others; that when improperly used it is capable of producing more evil than good; that the decision to criminalize any particular behavior must follow only after an assessment and balancing of gains and losses—this obvious injunction of rationality has been noted widely for over 250 years, from Jeremy Bentham, to the National Crime Commission, and by the moralistic philosophers as well as the utilitarian ones. [Prof. Sanford H. Kadish, "The Crisis of Overcriminalization," 7 *American Criminal Law Quarterly* 17, 33 (Fall 1968).

Vagrancy. (1) The following described persons are guilty of vagrancy and shall be punished upon conviction by imprisonment in the county jail for a period not exceeding six months, or by a fine of not more than $100, or both:

a. Every person without visible means of living, who has the physical ability to work, and who does not for the space of 10 days seek employment, nor labor when employment is offered him.

b. Every beggar who solicits alms as a business.

c. Every idle or dissolute person, or associate of known thieves, who wanders about the streets or highways at late or unusual hours of the night, or who lodges in any barn, shed, shop, out-house, vessel, car or place other than such as is kept for lodging purposes, without the permission of the owner or party entitled to the possession thereof.

d. Every common prostitute.

e. Any person who is not enrolled as a student or who is not employed by the public or private school and who, without lawful purpose therefore, wilfully loiters about any public or private school building or the public premises adjacent thereto.

f. Any person who conducts himself in a violent, riotous, or disorderly manner, or who uses abusive, obscene or profane language in a public place or upon any public highway, or in a house or place whereby the peace or quiet of the neighborhood or vicinity may be disturbed. [Section 166.060 of the Oregon Revised Statutes (1965)]

Most criminal laws proscribe actions which result in a direct and identifiable harm to another. Usually, the actor is subject to punishment only if he has acted knowingly, willfully, and intentionally. Murder, robbery, rape, arson, and embezzlement are typical examples. One or more victims suffer the consequences of another's antisocial conduct.

When, however, the criminal law begins to define certain petty offenses, this generalization is less applicable. There is not always a victim, or an identifiable harm, or an act that is knowing, willful and intentional, or even an act at all. These petty offenses fall roughly into three groups, each of which, to some degree, has an effect on the criminal process.

There are crimes without victims, acts which hurt no person in particular but offend society generally. Examples include laws against prostitution, abortion, homosexuality, gambling, obscenity, and possession (not sale) of narcotics.

There are also laws which do not punish action, but inaction, or the occupation of a particular status. Laws against public drunkenness and vagrancy are typical examples. Another popular law makes it a crime to be an able-bodied person with no visible means of support who does not seek work. See subsection 1 (a) of the Oregon statute at the beginning of the Chapter. The same statute maeks it a crime to be a "common prostitute." This is in addition to the crime of prostitution. The first punishes a status, the second an act.

In a third group are laws defining conduct that does affect others; but these laws are vague and overbroad and, consequently, give the police wide discretion and power in controlling on-the-street behavior. Examples include disorderly conduct and disturbing-the-peace statutes and prohibitions against offenses to the "common decency." Subsections 1 (c), (e) and (f) of the Oregon statute are examples of this use of vague language. What do "idle," "dissolute," "loiter," and "disorderly" mean?

It is beyond the scope of this book to consider the wisdom of victimless, status, and overbroad offenses, independent of their effect on the criminal process. However, if these substantive criminal laws were phenomenally successful in dealing with the social problems they define, we might be willing to endure their negative effect on the administration of criminal justice. But even a cursory review of the problem is enough to convince us that this is not so. The criminal law is used in these areas not for humanitarian ends but because it is the cheapest and most efficient method to control disagreeable minorities and unpleasant individuals. We want the drunk taken away when he strays into our neighborhood. We want the beggar locked up when he bothers us. We want the prostitutes—at least the ones who use the streets—arrested. We want the police to have the power to deal summarily with hippies, demonstrators, and other outsiders who threaten us. And if removal, rather than rehabilitation or reconciliation, is the goal, the criminal process is certainly cheap and efficient.

For example, a vagrant strays into a respectable, residential neighborhood and is arrested because he has committed the crime of being poor, able-bodied, and without a job. As soon as he is released, he is a recidivist and could be rearrested. Often the penalty is "$100 or ninety days." By definition a vagrant does not have $100; if he did, he'd be innocent. Arrested for his poverty, he is then sent to jail because he is too poor to pay the money that will keep him out. (This practice is now being challenged in the Supreme Court on equal protection and due process grounds.) The law has accomplished its goal—the vagrant is off the streets. The process is efficient because the goal was removal of the object, not rehabilitation of the person. The inescapable conclusion is that we use the criminal law to define victimless, status, and overbroad offenses precisely because they enable us (we shall discuss how) to circumvent due process requirements.

The scope of the problem is reflected in arrest statistics. The FBI's *Uniform Crime Reports* (1969) reports 5,773,988 arrests in areas covered by 4,759 enforcement agencies with a combined population of 143,815,000. This is a rate of 4,014.9 arrests per 100,000 people. Of these totals, the following crimes accounted for the indicated number of arrests:

Crime	Arrests	Rate per 100,000 of Population
Prostitution and commercialized vice	46,410	32.3
Sex offenses (except forcible rape and prostitution) [1]	50,143	34.9
Narcotic drug laws [2]	232,690	161.8
Gambling	78,020	54.3
Offenses against family and children [3]	50,312	35.0
Drunkenness	1,420,161	987.5
Disorderly conduct	573,503	398.8
Vagrancy	106,269	73.9
All other offenses (except traffic)	664,634	462.1
Suspicion [4]	88,265	61.4
Curfew and loitering (juveniles only) [5]	101,674	70.7
Runaways [5] (juveniles only)	156,468	110.9

[1] For example, statutory rape, offenses against chastity, common decency, morals, etc.

[2] Includes both sale and possession of both "hard" and "soft" drugs. This category has increased from 69.3 per 100,000 in 1967.

[3] For example, nonsupport, neglect and desertion.

[4] Some jurisdictions permit arrest on suspicion. This gives police virtually unlimited discretion to place a person in custody.

[5] The rates for these offenses are misleadingly low because they are per 100,000 population, not per 100,000 juveniles.

More than half of all arrests are for minor crimes. Some of these have no victims. Others involve no antisocial action. And still others are defined by overbroad statutes which permit the arresting officer to fill in the blanks.

How are status, nonvictim, and overbroad offenses used (legally and illegally) to circumvent the rules due process requires? How do these laws affect law enforcement?

In Chapter 4 we said the police could search a person after a lawful arrest. In addition, a policeman may lawfully arrest without an arrest warrant if there is probable cause to believe that an offense is being committed in his presence. In a jurisdiction that prohibits, for example, loitering about private places with-

out permission, a policeman may arrest if he sees a person
loitering about a private place and he has probable cause to believe the owner has not given his permission. And anything the
policeman finds in the ensuing search is competent evidence,
even if it has no connection with the crime for which the suspect
was arrested and even if the suspect is acquitted of the loitering
charge.

Similarly, a policeman can arrest under subsection 1 (c) of
the Oregon statute if a suspect wanders about the street at an
"unusual" hour and the policeman has probable cause to believe the suspect is "idle or dissolute."

A shabbily dressed person in a middle-class neighborhood
may be removed under some laws if he is "unable to account
for his presence."

If a group of people congregate on the street, they may be
dispersed under a statute that requires them to move on after
receiving a "lawful" order to do so. Or they could be arrested
if the arresting officer determines they are "disorderly" or that
a "breach of the peace may be occasioned."

Policemen can use laws against prostitution, public drunkenness and homosexuality as neighborhood controls or during pe-
riodic "wars" on homosexuals, prostitutes, or bums.

If a group of young people sit in a park and play musical instruments on a Sunday afternoon, the police can end the conduct by deciding that the young people are disorderly or that
their music disturbs the peace.

With little difficulty, a creative and patient policeman will be
able to find some valid ground to arrest and search, if that is his
goal. Under traditional due process safeguards, a law officer
cannot order a person to go back where he comes from or be
arrested. But laws that define status and victimless crimes permit just that. Nor does due process permit arrest without cause.
But laws that broadly define varieties of conduct and allow
policemen to provide the detail effectively permit arrests with
little or no cause.

Many people loiter about private places without permission. Many wander on the streets at unusual hours. Such behavior is innocuous in most cases. And, of course, most people are not arrested for these acts. If they were, the law would quickly be changed. But the power that these laws give to policemen is not usually used against respectable, middle-class people. It is used selectively, against particular outcast groups and disagreeable minorities.

In his book, *Police Power: Police Abuses in New York City*[1], Paul Chevigny concludes, after a two-year study of a large number of petty criminal cases, that police use their discretionary powers against people who are defiant or disrespectful of their authority. Generally, too, the victims of police arbitrariness are members of outcast groups, toward whom the policeman feels disdain or hostility. Chevigny found that members of these groups threaten the policeman's authority by their very existence; unlike persons in the mainstream, they incur police antagonism without any affirmative action. Hippies, homosexuals, political activists (generally on the left), derelicts, prostitutes, and narcotics users are particularly susceptible to police reprisals.

After a policeman arrests someone who challenges his authority, Chevigny found, he may use other legal sanctions to cover his mistake. If the officer injures the suspect, there may be a charge of resisting arrest to explain the injury. If the policeman wants bargaining power at the trial, he may add a felonious assault charge. The bargaining begins when the prosecutor concludes he does not have a case. He may then offer to drop the resisting arrest and felonious assault charges if the defendant pleads guilty to the offense for which he was originally arrested —usually disturbing the peace. Or the prosecutor may be willing to drop all charges in exchange for an agreement not to sue the city or the policeman for false arrest.

[1] Paul Chevigny, *Police Power: Police Abuses in New York City* (New York: Pantheon Books, 1969).

We expect that when policemen misuse the criminal law, supervisory personnel will respond to these abuses. However, Chevigny found that the New York Police Review Board was unwilling to punish a policeman for doing his job too industriously. If the excesses were in the line of duty, they were excusable.

Another check on police abuse of the criminal process is the court system. If a policeman arrests because he deems certain conduct disorderly, a judge will eventually be able to determine whether the conduct was, in fact, proscribed by the law. However, even this check is not entirely effective because, as Chevigny discovered, the police are willing to lie about events leading up to an arrest. In the eyes of the police, the outcasts with whom they deal have a guilty intent anyway, even if they did not actually commit a crime. They are potential offenders, so that arrest, and distortion of the facts to cover the arrest, is morally, if not legally, proper. (In some cases, an arrest—particularly an unjustified arrest of a member of an outcast group—can escalate to physical violence.) Later, in court, the defendant will find it next to impossible to disprove the policeman's version of the facts. The judge is more likely to believe the "disinterested" policeman than the accused.

But even if the policeman is completely honest in relating the conduct he believed was disorderly, the court disagrees, and the accused is acquitted, problems remain. There is the inconvenience of the arrest. The accused may actually have spent one or more nights in jail if he could not immediately raise bail. He may lose his job or several days' pay. The arrest may embarrass him within his community or before his family. He may have to wait weeks or months until the matter is finally settled and he is vindicated. Throughout, there is the possibility that he will eventually have to go to jail or pay a fine. If he does not lose his job after the initial arrest, he'll need an understanding boss because there'll be many court appearances before the final disposition of his case. A lawyer has to be paid. Finally, after it is all over and he is acquitted, the accused will still have to affirmatively answer that perennial question: "Have you ever been arrested?" All these consequences could be avoided if petty offense statutes were more specific and, therefore, abuse of police discretion less likely.

The President's Crime Commission corroborates some of Chevigny's conclusions.[2] The Commission reported that:

Minor crime statutes are frequently misused. They are employed as a means of clearing undesirables or unsightly persons from the street or driving them out of town, aiding the police in detaining a suspected person during an investigation of a more serious crime, and regulating street activity in slum neighborhoods. Often, under pressure from the community, the police will "declare a war on bums, prostitutes, homosexuals, and narcotic traffickers" by making wholesale arrests for vagrancy, disorderly conduct, drunkenness, or loitering.

The Commission continued:

Most statutes which are used to regulate street conduct are so broad that almost unlimited discretion is given to the police officer to arrest persons on the street or, as with a failure-to-move-on statute, to regulate conduct by the threat of arrest. Such statutes should be amended to cover only conduct which reasonably disturbs the public or is an immediate threat to the peace. Even if this is done, however, there would still be a need for police departments to formulate guidelines concerning their permissible use. The guidelines should clearly bar discriminatory enforcement of minor crime statutes either against individuals or in particular neighborhoods.

To some extent, of course, it is difficult to draw a criminal statute narrowly when the crime is disorderly conduct or dis-

[2] The President's Commission on Law Enforcement and Administration of Justice, Task Force on the Police (1967).

turbing the peace. Language also has its limits, and policemen must have some discretion in order to handle the great variety of on-the-street encounters. Ultimately, dishonesty and abuses of discretion will be eliminated if better working conditions attract more qualified men and women to law enforcement. However, as the Commission suggested, legislatures could and should specify the conduct that concerns them and, so far as possible, not leave that determination to the individual officer's discretion. In addition, police departments can orally inform the man on the beat exactly what kind of activity does and what kind does not require an official response. Following is a section from the American Law Institute's Model Penal Code.[3] Compare its specificity with the Oregon law at the beginning of the Chapter.

Section 250.6 Loitering or Prowling

A person commits a violation if he loiters or prowls in a place, at a time, or in a manner not usual for law-abiding individuals under circumstances that warrant alarm for the safety of persons or property in the vicinity. Among the circumstances which may be considered in determining whether such alarm is warranted is the fact that the actor takes flight upon appearance of a peace officer, refuses to identify himself, or manifestly endeavors to conceal himself or any object. Unless flight by the actor or other circumstances make it impracticable, a peace officer shall prior to any arrest for an offense under this section afford the actor an opportunity to dispel any alarm which would otherwise be warranted, by requesting him to identify himself and explain his presence and conduct. No person shall be convicted of an offense under this Section if the peace officer did not comply with the preceding sentence, or if it appears at trial that the explanation given by the actor was true and, if believed by the peace officer at the time, would have dispelled the alarm.

[3] American Law Institute, *Model Penal Code* (Proposed Official Draft, May 4, 1962).

Judicial Reaction

The Supreme Court's rulings in the petty criminal law area
are few and inconclusive. In *Robinson* v. *California.* 370 U.S.
660 (1962), the Court held that it was cruel and unusual
punishment and in violation of the Eighth Amendment, to make
the "status" of being a narcotic addict a crime. Sale or possession of narcotics may still be prohibited. But when California
tried to criminally punish someone for being in a condition
where he was addicted to narcotics, the Court said no. In
Powell v. *Texas,* 392 U.S. 514 (1968), a five-man majority,
refusing to extend *Robinson,* upheld the conviction of a chronic
alcoholic for the crime of public drunkenness. Justice Fortas,
dissenting, argued that *Robinson* does not permit inflicting
criminal penalties on a person who is "in a condition he is
powerless to change." But Justice Marshall, writing for four
members of the Court, said Powell's punishment was not for
"being a chronic alcoholic" but "for being in public while drunk
on a particular occasion." Justice White, whose concurrence
provided a bare majority, explained his vote by contending
that Powell evidently could have avoided being drunk in public.
The case is not notable for its incisive reasoning. The 5–4 split
suggests that the next few years might see developments in this
area, though probably not from the Burger Court.

In 1966, the Supreme Court agreed to review a vagrancy
statute that was attacked on constitutional grounds. However,
the Court later changed its mind and withdrew its grant of review. Justice Douglas dissented from this about-face and excerpts from his dissent follow.[4]

---

[4] The case is *Hicks* v. *District of Columbia,* 383 U.S. 252 (1966). The
statute under which the Petitioner had been convicted defined a "vagrant" as

Any person leading an immoral or profligate life who has no lawful employment and who has no lawful means of support realized from a lawful occupation or source.

Our vagrancy laws stem from the series of the Statutes of Labourers . . . first passed in 1349 and amended and modified from time to time over the next 200 years. They reflected "the criminal aspect of the poor laws." They "confined the labouring population to stated places of abode, and required them to work at specified rates of wages. Wandering or vagrancy thus became a crime." History tells the story from the point of view of the Establishment: that wandering bands of people, who had left their masters, committed all sorts of crimes and hence must be punished for wandering. That philosophy obtains in this country, because the English statutes provided the seed of our vagrancy laws. Article IV, ᶜ 1, of the Articles of Confederation assured the free inhabitants of each State, save "paupers, vagabonds, and fugitives from Justice," the privileges and immunities of citizenship of the several States, and the right of free ingress and egress to and from each State.

But there was incongruity in superimposing the English antimigratory policy upon the law of America:

> "Vast movements of people motivated by urgent economic need settled this country from Europe, pushed settlement westward and fed growing cities from rural population reservoirs. England's Enclosure Acts, by withdrawing land from agricultural use, swelled the army of English vagrants; America invited migration with the lure of free land. The same elements of the population who on one side of the Atlantic were rogues and vagabonds, on the other were frontiersmen."

America's vagrancy laws were expanded to cover a host of acts other than wandering—begging, drunkenness, disorderly conduct, loitering, prostitution, lewdness, narcotics peddling, and so on. They were justified here, as in early England, as devices of control. This Court, writing in 1837, said:

> "We think it as competent and as necessary for a state to provide precautionary measures against the moral pestilence of paupers, vagabonds, and possibly convicts; as it is to guard against the physical pestilence, which may arise from unsound and infectious articles imported, or from a ship, the crew of which may be labouring under an infectious disease." . . .

The wanderer, the pauper, the unemployed—all were deemed to be potential criminals. As stated by the Court of Appeals for the

District of Columbia Circuit in *District of Columbia* v. *Hunt*, . . . "A vagrant is a probable criminal; and the purpose of the statute is to prevent crimes which may likely flow from his mode of life." The vagrant, therefore, is not necessarily one who has committed any crime but one who reflects "a present condition or status." . . . That condition is not a failure to make a productive contribution to society, for the idle rich are not reached. The idle pauper is the target. Insofar as that status reflects pauperism it suggests the need for welfare; and insofar as it reflects idleness it suggests the need for the intervention of employment agencies. I do not see how under our constitutional system either of those elements can be made a crime. To do so serves the cause either of arrests and convictions on suspicion or of arrests and convictions of unpopular minorities . . . —procedures very convenient to the police but foreign to our system.

I do not see how economic or social status can be made a crime any more than being a drug addict can be. . . . No overt act of criminal dimensions is charged here. Petitioner was either arrested on suspicion or for innocent acts which were used as a cloak for an arrest on grounds the police could not establish. In either event the arrest and conviction were, in my view, unconstitutional.

Every jurisdiction has some kind of vagrancy law. In *Fenster* v. *Leary,* 20 N.Y.2d 309 (1967), the New York Court of Appeals declared the New York vagrancy statute unconstitutional. Since then, a small number of other courts have followed *Fenster.*

Three times in two months Charles Fenster was arrested under the New York vagrancy law. That law defined as a vagrant "a person who, not having visible means to maintain himself, lives without employment." Fenster was acquitted each time. The Court's opinion does not say so, but probably Fenster believed, with some justification, that the police were using the vagrancy statute to intentionally harass him. Eventually, Fenster brought an action to declare the law unconstitutional. Excerpts from the opinion of the New York Court of Appeals striking down the statute follow:

[W]e feel the statute is defective on the ground that, whatever purpose and role it may or may not have served in an earlier day, and however valid or invalid may be the proposition that the able-bodied unemployed poor are a likely source of crime, in this era of widespread efforts to motivate and educate the poor toward economic betterment of themselves, of the "War on Poverty" and all its varied programs, it is obvious to all that the vagrancy laws have been abandoned by our governmental authorities as a means of "persuading" unemployed poor persons to seek work (the Attorney General does not even suggest that the vagrancy laws would be invoked against such people today). It is also obvious that today the only persons arrested and prosecuted as common-law vagrants are alcoholic derelicts and other unfortunates, whose only crime, if any, is against themselves, and whose main offense usually consists in their leaving the environs of skid row and disturbing by their presence the sensibilities of residents of nicer parts of the community, or suspected criminals, with respect to whom the authorities do not have enough evidence to make a proper arrest or secure a conviction on the crime suspected.

As to the former, it seems clear that they are more properly objects of the welfare laws and public health programs than of the criminal law and, as to the latter, it should by now be clear to our governmental authorities that the vagrancy laws were never intended to be and may not be used as an administrative short cut to avoid the requirements of constitutional due process in the administration of criminal justice. If it is only to allow arrests and criminal prosecutions for vagrancy to continue against individuals such as these that the Attorney General would have us uphold the statute, then it must fall. And despite certain fairly recent cases upholding similar statutes . . . we can, in fact, see no other purpose in our statute today and, therefore, find it invalid.

The Balance

We have seen how overcriminalization may be used, legally and otherwise, to avoid adherence to due process guarantees. We have also noted the general reluctance, with few exceptions, of the Supreme Court and other courts to interfere in this area. Perhaps the courts will refuse to second-guess the legislatures until the irrationality and uselessness of criminally defining certain "antisocial" conduct is so clearly proved that the practice can safely be called "unconstitutional." I cannot here provide that proof, but, as the following article suggests, I think serious arguments can be made that many petty offense statutes are productive of no social good for either the state or the accused and are a strikingly foolish way to respond to the conduct they define:[5]

I

New York City dispenses justice as mechanically and impersonally as it dispenses traffic tickets or welfare checks.

It is true that the quality of the justice dispensed is high and that is important. But it is not likely that the accused citizen, winding his way through the City's criminal courts, will believe this— and that is equally important.

Part IC defendants are not the professional criminal, the felon, the organized criminal. Part IC defendants are borderline members of society, people who are part in and part alienated, people who are generally charged with petty violations—disturbing the peace, refusal to disperse—or social crimes—prostitution, drunken driving—acts that perhaps should not be criminal at all. It is essential that society impress such people with its concern that they be given a fair day in court. This it does not do.

II

The criminal process in Part 1C is unintelligible to the layman accused of a crime. He is an object moving along a conveyor belt, pelted now and then with questions, with directions, with instructions, all of which, at the end of the process, are supposed to add up to justice. To his lawyer it probably will. To lawyers justice is defined in terms of process, due process. But to the accused justice is the gut feeling he has after it's all over: he got a fair shake or he did not. And if he feels he did not, that's one more push toward greater alienation and perhaps more antisocial behavior (and serious crime) and it will help not at all to tell him about the due process he received. He hasn't understood a thing that went on.

III

Part 1C is located on the second floor of 100 Centre Street.

[5] Reprinted from *The Commentator*, 2, no. 12 (March 13, 1968) p. 1.

Every weekday morning dozens of people, some with lawyers, some without, mill around the entrance to Part 1C, the beginning of the conveyor belt. These people come in response to a summons, they are trusted to appear. Others, who are not trusted to appear and who cannot post the necessary bail, are brought, from jail, to a room behind the courtroom. The room is called the cage and that is where they wait for justice. Because there is only one cage, women who are in custody are permitted to sit on a reserved bench in the courtroom.

IV

Most of the women are prostitutes. Most of the prostitutes are Negro or Puerto Rican. Almost all are streetwalkers. Expensive call-girls rarely come to Part 1C. They are rarely arrested, rarely receive a summons. It is only the woman who walks the street because she must—for the money—whom the law is able to catch.

Every morning you can see a dozen or so prostitutes at Part 1C. Some are newcomers but most are repeaters. It's just another stop on the merry-go-round in an absurd game. No one can even pretend there's any rational connection between a prostitute's occasional appearances at 100 Centre Street and justice. Part 1C is an occupational hazard, costing both the streetwalker and the City time and money, and helping neither.

The maximum sentence now is 3 months. The convicted prostitute will spend her time at the Women's House of Detention in Greenwich Village, described, in assorted articles, as being a hellhole at best. No attempt is made to help her. No one offers to relieve her of the economic pressures that force her onto the streets. Instead, the People, in their Courts of Law, pronounce her a criminal and send her away. Certainly, she is less guilty than her accusers.

V

The hallways outside Part 1C happen to be, logically enough, the place where two groups of people tend to congregate. Pimps and lawyers. A pimp may be there because one of his girls has been pulled in. Or, very likely, he is there because what better place in New York is there to meet and recruit new girls?

The lawyers who hang around the hallways outside Part 1C are something else again. Some, though, I emphasize, not all, are looking for clients. They are a discredit to their profession, but no one pretends otherwise. What's worse is the treatment they give clients they happen to find.

These lawyers have no office. Perhaps there is a place they receive mail. Their fee, very often, is whatever the prospective client has on him. The client is often a member of a minority group. He (or she) is glad to get a white lawyer. He is sure that whatever he gets would have been worse if he did not have the white lawyer. The lawyer does little for his money. He will plead his client guilty, offer extenuating circumstances. Rarely will a case go to trial. One wonders if some of the lawyers who hang around 100 Centre Street know the rules of evidence.

VI

The courtroom that is Part 1C is a large, dim place. On the front wall, above the judge's chair, is written "In God We Trust." The first rows on either side of the room are reserved for police officers and attorneys. The other rows are for defendants, their friends and families, the public. It is nearly impossible to hear anything that is happening up front. Trials in that room cannot seriously be called public.

Up front, near the judge, is a stenographer, a clerk of the court, about a half dozen additional clerks to handle the voluminous amount of paperwork and peopledirecting, the assistant DA, and the Legal Aid Lawyer. The Legal Aid Lawyer has no name. He is called Legal Aid. The City has an arrangement whereby the Legal Aid Society defends all indigent defendants.

There is no jury. New York law guarantees a jury only if the crime charged is punishable by more than one year in jail. If it is punishable by 15 days or less, the defendant is entitled to be tried by one judge. If the punishment can be longer than 15 days, he is entitled to three judges. [*Baldwin* v. *New York* has changed this.]

VII

For the most part, the criminal court judges are competent, sympathetic men and the faults in the City's criminal system do not lie with them.

The judges in the criminal court are appointed by the mayor. Mayor Lindsay has just reappointed all but one of Mayor Wagner's old appointments. They are paid $30,000 a year. It is an awful job. They write no opinions and are, in fact, urged not to. They have no law clerks to help them. They often must work nights, weekends, holidays, and they dread being assigned to Staten Island. Innumerable people want the job.

VIII

There is currently before the Supreme Court of the United States a case which asks that the federal guarantee to a jury trial in criminal cases be applied to the states. New York City has filed an *amicus* brief claiming that if the federal right is applied to the states in its totality, it would put the City out of business. Indeed it might. The City could never handle the load it does if juries had to be called for every trial. One thousand people are arrested in Manhattan every single day. If only a small per cent of these requested jury trials, the cost in money and time would be huge.

On the other hand, if the City were subject to the jury requirement, perhaps it would slow things down enough to make the criminal process more intelligible to the accused citizen. Now, with the accent on efficiency and disposition of as many cases as possible, a man can find himself locked up and fined without really understanding what went on.

IX

Every time a defendant appears at 100 Centre Street the complaining police officer must also be present, whether or not he's needed. Consequently, one can see dozens of policemen there any morning, wearing civilian clothing, but careful to have their badges pinned to their sweaters for identification. It is possibly the greatest single instance of manpower waste in the city. The Mayor has said he is going to change it, but nothing has been done yet.

X

The routine is interesting at first. The criminal process in motion! But after a while the assembly line aspects of it become apparent. It becomes dull, repetitive, automatic. The process is there —in full—but substance is entirely lacking.

"James Smith," the clerk calls. A man comes forward.

"James Smith?"

"Yes."

"Where's your lawyer?" the judge asks.

Smith shakes his head.

"Do you have a lawyer?"

"No."

"Can you afford a lawyer?"

"No."

"Legal Aid assigned."

And so on. Legal Aid can get an extension if he needs one, but probably, after a short conference, the case will be tried that very day.

XI

The concern with whether the accused has a lawyer and with

procedure generally is, of course, a result of *Escobedo* and *Miranda,* and other cases which emphasize that the quality of the process is the determinant of the constitutionality of the justice. But I think there is another reason, too.

Fairness, for the Law, is a procedural concept. But for the accused, fairness is a question of whether he deserves to be punished and process is unimportant. The Law and the accused do not speak the same language. Factors one may deem relevant the other may be totally unconcerned with.

Therefore, to keep things running smoothly, it is in the interest of the system to make certain the accused has a lawyer, someone who speaks the same language as the court, someone whose presence can justify keeping the accused himself out of the criminal process. But while the Law may feel satisfied that it has given a man his due process before sending him away, the accused, on the other hand, may never have been questioned about those aspects of his case that he feels must be known before he can fairly be judged guilty or innocent, before society can say he deserves to be punished. The consequences of such a situation are all the more grave since a citizen convicted in Part 1C is often not a "criminal" in any legitimate sense of the word.

XII

What we are doing, then, is using the criminal process in response to the largely antisocial—and not really criminal—activity of certain segments of our population. That many of the accused who stream daily through Part 1C can readily be identified as belonging to particular "segments" of society corroborates the contention that the violating conduct is more antisocial than criminal.

I do not suggest, generally, that our use of the criminal law is a political response to control specific groups or classes in society. But the result is the same whatever may be our motives. The result is a gross inefficiency in human terms, in terms of human accomplishment. The great cost in time, labor, and money does not produce the change in the quality of life that should be our goal. Our treatment of prostitutes most blatantly illustrates this inefficiency. But it is not unique.

Like a great net the law enforcement industry sweeps across the precincts of the City and pulls in the alienated, the poor, the discriminated against, the angry, and the broken.

In Part 1C the accused finds the Law unconcerned with his life, interested only in the particular conduct which has brought him there. He may not understand how his conduct can be considered apart from his life. He finds himself in an adversary system he does not comprehend, being attacked in ways he does not know how to defend against.

Meanwhile, the Law punishes the convicted citizen on the naive assumption that punishment, more than assistance, will deter future illegal conduct, that the accused was a free agent who voluntarily broke a rule, and that it is necessary to the system that he be obliged to pay his debt to society.

It seems to me the obligations run the other way around.

Police Lawlessness

The constitutional rules of criminal procedure will only be meaningful if they are observed. Ultimately, the vitality of the criminal process as a rule-oriented one depends on the honesty of the people charged with its enforcement. Two types of police misconduct that threaten the proper administration of the criminal law are (1) distortion or suppression of facts in order to assure conviction, and (2) disregard of individual rights to achieve a goal other than conviction.

(1) *Distortion or Suppression of Facts in Order to Assure Conviction*

In certain cases the police will lie in order to assure a conviction at trial. Additional inducements might include avoidance of a possible reprimand or a civil suit for false arrest. Misrepresentation is necessarily accompanied by a disregard of the defendant's rights. If the misrepresentation concerns the facts of the alleged criminal activity (rather than the arrest or search), conviction and punishment of an innocent person may result. If the policeman contradicts the defendant, the judge will generally believe the policeman. The ostensible explanation is that the defendant has more reason to lie. This, of course, is not always true because a policeman who has intentionally ignored a suspect's rights may find himself in trouble if the truth is discovered.

The cases Chevigny documents provide abundant data for a conclusion that the police frequently misrepresent the factual circumstances surrounding an arrest or search. It is not certain how often this occurs. Certainty would require a careful study, and that is not likely so long as there is official reluctance to admit that the problem exists.[6] In addition, a policeman is not likely to admit he perjured himself to get a conviction. Nevertheless, Chevigny and others[7] have supplied information which suggests that the problem is sizable and certainly serious enough to evoke official concern. In addition, strong negative attitudes toward the police in ghetto neighborhoods should make an objective observer incredulous of any claim that these attitudes stem wholly from the residents' imaginations.

A partial explanation of police misconduct is that law officers only do what society asks. Indeed, the courts (at least the lower ones) pretend constitutional guarantees prevail, while tacitly ignoring less egregious transgressions. In this way, we are able to live in two different worlds: we can preach the Bill of Rights but practice police power.

Police departments are not composed of unique men and women. Law enforcers draw their values and attitudes from the society in which they live. If policemen lie, they do so partially

[6] Chevigny could not get cooperation from the New York City Police Department for his study.

[7] See Jerome Skolnick, *Justice Without Trial* (New York: Wiley, 1966); the same author has written a report for the President's Commission on the Causes and Prevention of Violence—*The Politics of Protest* (New York: Ballantine, 1969); Arthur Niederhoffer, *Behind the Shield: Police in Urban Society* (New York: Doubleday, 1969); Selwyn Raab, *Justice in the Back Room* (Cleveland: World, 1967); Daniel Walker, *Rights in Conflict* (New York: Dutton, 1969); Archibald Cox, *Crisis at Columbia* (New York: Vintage, 1968).

because they believe they should, that they are expected to, that it is right. Private citizens must examine their own expectations and beliefs. Like many other legal issues, there is an underlying political question here: In a constitutional democracy, what is the role of the police? Do we want the policeman to alter a minor fact or two in order to assure conviction of the rapist or burglar? Or do we want him to tell the truth even if the court will then be forced to acquit the defendant?

The following article by Professor (now Judge) Irving Younger examines this problem and offers some explanations. The article was written shortly after the Supreme Court decided *McCray* v. *Illinois,* discussed in Chapter 4.

THE PERJURY ROUTINE[8]

On March 20, in *McCray* v. *Illinois* the Supreme Court held that when, on being questioned as to whether there was probable cause to arrest a defendant, a policeman testifies that a "reliable informant" told him that the defendant was committing a crime, the policeman need not name the informant. Justice Stewart, for himself and four other members of the Court, said that "nothing in the Due Process Clause of the Fourteenth Amendment requires a state court judge in every such hearing to assume the arresting officers are committing perjury."

Why not? Every lawyer who practices in the criminal courts knows that police perjury is commonplace.

The reason is not hard to find. Policemen see themselves as fighting a two-front war—against criminals in the street and against "liberal" rules of law in court. All's fair in this war, including the use of perjury to subvert "liberal" rules of law that might free those who "ought" to be jailed. And even if his lies are exposed in the courtroom, the policeman is as likely to be indicted for perjury by his co-worker, the prosecutor, as he is to be struck down by thunderbolts from an avenging heaven.

It is a peculiarity of our legal system that the police have unique opportunities (and unique temptations) to give false testimony. When the Supreme Court lays down a rule to govern the conduct

[8] By Irving Younger. Reprinted from the *Nation,* May 8, 1967, p. 596.

of the police, the rule does not enforce itself. Some further proceeding, such as the "probable cause" hearing in *McCray*, is almost always necessary to determine what actually happened. In *Mapp* v. *Ohio*, for example, the Supreme Court laid down the rule that evidence obtained by the police through an unreasonable search and seizure may not be used in a state criminal prosecution. But before applying the rule to any particular case, a hearing must be held to establish the facts. Then the judge decides whether those facts constitute an unreasonable search and seizure. In *Miranda* v. *Arizona*, the Court held that a suspect must be fully warned of his right to remain silent and to the assistance of counsel before his statements will be admissible against him. But in any particular case, as under *Mapp*, a hearing must first be held to determine whether the suspect was in fact properly warned. Only if the judge concludes that he was properly warned do his statements come into evidence against him.

Such hearings usually follow a standard pattern. The policemen testify to their version of the circumstances of the search or of the interrogation, always reflecting perfect legality. The defendant testifies to his version, always reflecting egregious illegality. The judge must choose between two statements, and, not surprisingly, he almost always accepts the policeman's word.

The difficulty arises when one stands back from the particular case and looks at a series of cases. It then becomes apparent that policemen are committing perjury at least in some of them, and perhaps in nearly all of them. Narcotics prosecutions in New York City can be so viewed. Before *Mapp*, the policeman typically testified that he stopped the defendant for little or no reason, searched him, and found narcotics on his person. This had the ring of truth. It was an illegal search (not based upon "probable cause"), but the evidence was admissible because *Mapp* had not yet been decided. Since it made no difference, the policeman testified truthfully. After the decision in *Mapp*, it made a great deal of difference. For the first few months, New York policemen continued to tell the truth about the circumstances of their searches, with the result that evidence was suppressed. Then the police made the great discovery that if the defendant drops the narcotics on the ground, after which the policeman arrests him, then the search is reasonable and the evidence is admissible. Spend a few hours in the New York City Criminal Court nowadays, and you will hear case after case in which a policeman testifies that the defendant dropped the narcotics on the ground, whereupon the policeman arrested him. Usually the very language of the testimony is identical from one case to another.

This is now known among defense lawyers and prosecutors as "dropsy" testimony. The judge has no reason to disbelieve it in any particular case, and of course the judge must decide each case on its own evidence, without regard to the testimony in other cases. Surely, though, not in *every* case was the defendant unlucky enough to drop his narcotics at the feet of a policeman. It follows that at least in some of these cases the police are lying.

Precisely because a judge is limited to the evidence in the particular case before him, judicial recognition of the problem of police perjury is extremely rare. It happened in 1965, however, in the United States Court of Appeals for the District of Columbia. In *Veney* v. *United States*,[9] the prosecutor offered evidence that each defendant had spontaneously apologized to the victim. Such spontaneous apologies had, six years before, been held admissible despite unlawful delay in arraigning the defendant. Judge J. Skelly Wright, in a concurring opinion, wrote:

> For some time now I have been curious and concerned about evidence offered by the Government, appearing again and again in criminal case records, showing that the defendant, at the lineup or other confrontation with the complaining witness, had, while in the presence and custody of the police, "spontaneously and voluntarily" apologized for his misdeed. The word "apologize" would not ordinarily be expected to be in the vocabularies of most of the poorly educated defendants. And even if it were, it seemed more than passing strange, to me at least, that this phenomenon of contrition should assert itself so soon after the offensive act. I began a search to solve the mystery. My efforts were first rewarded by my discovery of the case [*in which the court had held spontaneous apologies by defendants admissible despite delay in arraigning them*]. . . . Since our ruling in [*that case*], and particularly in the more recent past, "spontaneous" apologies by defendants have been offered by the Government and received in evidence in criminal cases with unusual frequency—usually supported by testimony that the apologies were not suggested or inspired by the police. . . . In view of the above, it appears to me that the time is ripe for some soul

9 344 F.2d 542 (1965).

searching in the prosecutor's office before it offers any more "spontaneous" apologies in evidence.

This year has also seen the beginning of official attempts to cope with the problem of police perjury. In March, 1966, the American Law Institute promulgated a Model Code of Pre-Arraignment Procedure, which provides that the police must make a tape recording of their questioning of an arrested person in order "to help eliminate factual disputes concerning what was said." More recently, the 20th police precinct in New York City has begun to tape-record all interviews with suspects.

But there will be no tape recordings on the streets, and perhaps the Supreme Court in *McCray* should not so casually have rejected the idea of a constitutional presumption that policemen commit perjury. There is ample factual basis for the presumption, and the courts, despite their reticence, are no strangers to those facts. Indeed, the dissenters in *McCray* hinted as much when they pointed out that "it is not unknown for the arresting officer to misrepresent his connection with the informer, his knowledge of the informer's reliability, or the information allegedly obtained from the informer."

Far from adopting a presumption of perjury, the *McCray* case almost guarantees wholesale police perjury. When his conduct is challenged as constituting an unreasonable search and seizure, all the policeman need say is that an unnamed "reliable informant" told him that the defendant was committing a crime. Henceforth, every policeman will have a genie-like informer to legalize his master's arrests.

This affronts the dignity of the administration of justice. And since there will now always be an informer to establish "probable cause," hence making all searches and seizures reasonable and all evidence admissible, however obtained, *McCray* marks the end of the short life of *Mapp* v. *Ohio*.

(2) Disregard of Individual Rights to Assure a Goal Other Than Conviction

A second problem concerns police misconduct that is not conviction-oriented. If a policeman violates an individual's rights and the truth is discovered, an exclusionary rule may prevent introduction of the tainted evidence in court. But, as Chief Justice Warren wrote in *Terry* v. *Ohio,* the exclusionary rule will not control police misconduct that is not conviction-oriented. Thus, to the extent that the police envision their role as other than catching and prosecuting criminals, the exclusionary rule is an ineffective check on misbehavior.

What function do police perform? Clearly the police must attempt to solve particular, reported crimes. They must also "police" public places and watch for crimes in progress or suspicious situations which may require additional investigation or surveillance. Beyond these two functions, the policeman's role is not so clear.[10] As the "policing" task comes to deal less with serious offenses and more with petty and vague offenses, the policeman becomes an on-the-street authority. His job is no longer to solve crimes that have been committed or are in the process of commission. His job is to keep things quiet and orderly. Petty offense statutes further encourage this shift in roles from "crime-solving" to "behavior-control." Their existence provides the cop on the beat with an assortment of legal pretexts which may be used to make behavior-control seem like crime-solving. Nevertheless, because the goal is behavior-control, the loss of a conviction is unimportant.

Proof of the behavior-control function is not hard to find. Newspapers frequently report police attempts to clear neighborhoods of "undesirables." The goal is to clean up the neighborhood, and its guise is the criminal law. The motive is frequently mp aints from the "respectable" residents and businessmen in the area. Consider, for example, the following article from *The New York Times.*[11]

The police arrested 254 persons charged with crimes committed in Times Square area in the week from April 7 through last Sunday, a spokesman . . . reported Friday. The arrests were part of a

[10] I am speaking only of the policeman's role *vis à vis* crime.
[11] April 20, 1969, sec. 1, page 19, col. 1.

drive on street crimes in the area bounded by West 38th and 45th Streets and the Avenue of the Americas and Ninth Avenue.

Convictions in that week totalled 104, with 74 persons dismissed and 76 persons placed on bail or paroled, or whose cases were adjourned or their outcome not reported.

In the previous week, there were 253 arrests, 66 convictions, 79 dismissals and 108 cases adjourned or their outcomes not reported.

For the period from February 5 through last Sunday, there were 3,019 arrests, including 1,082 convictions, 854 dismissals and 1,083 cases in the final category.

Most of the arrests in the period April 7–13 occurred between 4 P.M. and 5 A.M. and included persons arrested for loitering, disorderly conduct, public intoxication, robbery or assault."

Nearly half the cases resulted in dismissal. This is a low batting average if the goal was conviction, but not if the goal was to clean up the neighborhood. In the latter case, the criterion for arrest would not be criminal activity, but the arresting officer's determination that the suspect's absence would make the neighborhood "cleaner." Conviction, if it subsequently occurs, is incidental.

Further proof that the police use the criminal law for reasons that have nothing to do with conviction comes from the 1968 Annual Report of the Criminal Court of the City of New York. In 1968 in New York City, of 5,721 arraignments for prostitution, 1,991 defendants were eventually discharged. (One wonders how many of those arrested were never even arraigned.) And of 16,051 arraignments for disorderly conduct, nearly half the defendants, 7,410, were discharged. On the other hand, for the comparatively specific violation of peddling, 15,300 of 16,140 arraigned defendants were ultimately convicted.

Finally, a recent report states that the district attorneys of New York City have told the police department that the "vast majority" of arrests for the crime of loitering for the purpose of unlawfully using or possessing a dangerous drug were "unwarranted and unfounded." During 1969, there were 13,304 such arrests in New York City, and 15,192 during the first eight months of 1970. A study indicated that about 89 percent of these arrests are eventually dismissed. As a result of this information, the City's police department instructed its officers to make no arrests for this offense "unless the circumstances are such to exclude every possible reason for [the suspect's] presence except such intent to use or possess dangerous drugs."[12]

Judicial Reaction

Mass arrests without regard to guilt can cause severe hardship to the victims of this police illegality. However, few such victims actually take the initiative and challenge the police practices in court. There are several reasons for this. First, the victims are not likely to view the courts as offering them protection. Second, since most harassment cases are isolated and accomplished events, court relief will have no prospective consequence. Finally, legal action is expensive and time-consuming. As a result, not many courts have ruled on the legality of an ongoing police department practice.

Occasionally, however, an individual or a group may request a court to enjoin continuous police misconduct. Two relatively recent cases in which this was done with some success are *Lankford* v. *Gelston*, 364 F.2d 197 (1966) and *Hughes* v. *Rizzo*, 282 F.Supp 881 (1968). The first case involves black residents in Baltimore; the second, hippies in Philadelphia.

In *Lankford* v. *Gelston,* the Baltimore police suspected Samuel and Earl Veney of robbing a liquor store and assaulting a police lieutenant. Warrants were secured for the Veneys' arrest and a special squad formed to find them.

---

[12] *The New York Times,* November 2, 1970, p. 49, cols. 5–8. It is this type of precise information which, if provided by the police department, can help the officer on the street in his attempt to define and apply vague criminal statutes.

In a nineteen-day period the police searched about 300 private residences without warrants. On every search, there was a police emergency vehicle carrying shotguns, submachine guns, tear-gas apparatus, and bulletproof vests. According to the Court, the searches were accomplished in the following way:

Four officers carrying shotguns or submachine guns and wearing bulletproof vests would go to the front door and knock. They would be accompanied or followed by supervising officers, a sergeant or lieutenant. Other men would surround the house, training their weapons on windows and doors. "As soon as an occupant opened the door, the first man would enter the house to look for any immediate danger, and the supervising officer would then talk to the person who had answered the door. Few stated any objection to the entry; some were quite willing to have the premises searched for the Veneys, while others acquiesced because of the show of force."

The Court then discussed two specific searches. Acting on a tip that the Veneys were staying with a family named Garrett, the police converged on the home of Samuel Lankford:

At 2 A.M. a search party led by the lieutenant knocked on the door, and Mrs. Lankford, awakened by the knock, opened the door. The officers entered the house and began their search while the lieutenant talked with the woman. She told him that her name was not Garrett. At the trial she denied that the officers asked for or were given permission to search, and [the lieutenant] acknowledged that his men had already gone to the second floor while he was talking with her. The husband was awakened in his second floor bedroom by two flashlights shining in his face and found four men with shotguns in his room. They questioned him, while other officers searched the remaining rooms including the children's bedrooms, and left.

In another instance, acting on an anonymous telephone call, fifteen policemen came to the house of Mr. and Mrs. Wallace at 9 P.M. one evening.

When the police arrived, Lucinda Wallace [an adult daughter] was showing slides to a group of her family and guests. Mr. and

Mrs. Wallace were both out, Mrs. Wallace at a beauty shop she operated four doors away. Six officers armed with shotguns and rifles entered and searched the home; others who were stationed outside would not allow Mrs. Wallace to enter and refused to explain what was happening. Reduced to tears, she was finally admitted to her home, where she was joined by her children, all crying hysterically. As the policemen were departing, they told Lucinda and her mother that they had received an anonymous call that the Veneys were in the house.

The Court, in granting an injunction prohibiting the police from conducting searches based only on uncorroborated anonymous tips, said:

This case reveals a series of the most flagrant invasions of privacy ever to come under the scrutiny of a federal court. The undisputed testimony indicates that the police in conducting the wholesale Veney raids were engaging in a practice which on a smaller scale has routinely attended efforts to apprehend persons accused of serious crime. If denying relief in these circumstances should be held a proper exercise of judicial restraint, it would be difficult to envision any case justifying judicial intervention. The parties seeking redress have committed no acts warranting violation of the privacy of their homes; there has never been any suspicion concerning them or their associations. It was not contended by the Attorney General, nor could it have been contended, that information from an anonymous and unverifiable source is probable cause for the search of a home.

Instances have often come to the attention of courts in which persons accused of crime have sought to prevent the use against them of illegally seized incriminating evidence. But it is only in the rare instance that a person not accused or even suspected of any crime petitions the court for redress of police invasion of his home. The reason is not that such invasions do not occur but, as Mr. Justice Jackson eloquently put it:

"Only occasional and more flagrant abuses come to the attention of the courts, and then only those where the search and seizure yields incriminating evidence and the defendant is at least sufficiently compromised to be indicted. If the officers raid a home, an office, or stop and search an automobile but find noth-

ing incriminating, this invasion of the personal liberty of the innocent too often finds no practical redress. There may be, and I am
convinced that there are, many unlawful searches of homes and
automobiles of innocent people which turn up nothing incriminating, in which no arrest is made, about which courts do nothing, and about which we never hear. . . ."

Baltimore City has escaped thus far the agony and brutality of
the riots experienced in New York City, Los Angeles, Chicago,
and other urban centers. Courts cannot shut their eyes to events
that have been widely publicized throughout the nation and the
world. Lack of respect for the police is conceded to be one of the
factors generating violent outbursts in Negro communities. The
invasions so graphically depicted in this case "could" happen in
prosperous surburban neighborhoods, but the innocent victims know
only that wholesale raids do not happen elsewhere and did happen
to them. Understandably they feel that such illegal treatment is
reserved for those elements who the police believe cannot or will
not challenge them. It is of the highest importance to community
morale that the Court shall give firm and effective reassurance,
especially to those who feel that they have been harassed by reason
of their color or their poverty.

Hughes v. *Rizzo* involved ongoing police harassment of
hippies in Philadelphia. The facts follow from the Court's
opinion:

On June 17, 1967, at about 9:15 P.M., members of the Philadelphia police department conducted a raid in the public park
known as Rittenhouse Square in the City of Philadelphia, and arrested approximately twenty-seven young persons, including the
plaintiffs, Hughes and Frederick. Those arrested were either "hippies," persons conversing with "hippies," or persons who sought to
protest, or make inquiries concerning, the arrests. All of the persons
arrested were transported in police vehicles to the police stationhouse at 13th and Thompson Streets, about eight or ten blocks
away from the scene of the arrests. All were photographed. All
were questioned, individually, by police officers; the questions included inquiries concerning "sexual orientation" and "political
affiliation." There were no questions concerning any alleged criminal conduct, but some of those arrested were asked general ques-

tions about possession and use of narcotics and dangerous drugs. Those arrested were detained at the police station for about an hour, and then released. No charges of any kind have been lodged against any of the persons arrested. The police photographs remain on file.

On July 5, 1967, at about 7:30 P.M., members of the Philadelphia police force again raided Rittenhouse Square and arrested approximately twenty young persons, including the plaintiff, Allen Saft. All of the persons arrested were transported in police vehicles to the police station-house located at 20th Street and Pennsylvania Avenue. There was some discussion concerning attitudes toward our policies in Viet Nam, but no questioning concerning any supposed criminal activity. No charges were lodged against any of the persons arrested. The draft-cards of some of the young men arrested had been confiscated at the time of the arrest; these were returned at the police-station. All those arrested were released.

At various other times during June and July, 1967, "hippies" and other young persons associating with "hippies" were taken into temporary custody by Fairmount Park guards in Rittenhouse Square. They were taken to the guardhouse located at one end of Rittenhouse Square, where they were searched and interrogated, and warned to stop frequenting Rittenhouse Square. Several were forced to leave the Square area, due to threats of physical violence by some Park guards; and many conventionally-dressed young persons were warned against any further contact or association with "hippies."

Some Park guards tend to discriminate against "hippies" in such matters as ordering them not to sit on certain walls or the perimeter of the pool in the Square (while permitting conventionally-dressed persons to do so); other Park guards do not discriminate against "hippies."

The mass arrests of June 17 and July 5 were totally unjustified. There is no evidence that the persons arrested were guilty of any improper conduct, nor did the police have any grounds for belief, or even suspicion, that those arrested were guilty of any crime.

At various times, juvenile runaways have been apprehended in Rittenhouse Square, and the police are constantly required to check the area for persons in that category. But this was not the purpose of the mass-arrests of June 17 and July 5; there was no probable cause to suppose that any of the persons arrested were runaway juveniles; and no comparison was made with any list of persons reported missing. Moreover, it is neither necessary nor reasonable to detain, transport, or interrogate young persons in order to ascertain whether they have been reported missing.

The constant presence of groups of "hippies" in Rittenhouse Square frequently acts as a deterrent to the use of the park by others, particularly elderly persons, having the same right to use the area as the "hippies."

No adequately-detailed regulations governing the conduct of persons in the Square or defining Where, particularly in reference to the pool area, persons may congregate, have been promulgated.

The Court acknowledged that there were social frictions and pressures between the hippies and the residents of the wealthy area surrounding Rittenhouse Square.

The police undoubtedly received complaints from area residents appalled by the sinister appearance of some "hippies" and the conduct ascribed to them. (For example, there is some suggestion in the testimony that on earlier occasions some "hippies" were guilty of swinging from trees, and similar boisterous conduct.) One can almost take judicial notice of the fact that many "hippies" experiment with narcotics and dangerous drugs. And the hearings in this case were persuasive that some are promiscuous; some are overtly homosexual; and some have so completely rejected the middle-class value of cleanliness that their very presence in the courtroom was an olfactory affront. These factors may help to explain, if not to legally justify, conduct by law-enforcement personnel which would otherwise be incredible.

But our criminal laws are directed toward actions, not status. . . . It is not a crime to be a "hippie," and the police could not lawfully arrest on the basis of suspicion, or even probable cause to believe, that the arrestee occupied the status of being a homosexual or narcotics addict. . . .

It is quite clear from the record in this case that the primary motive for the various arrests and interrogations referred to above was a desire to rid Rittenhouse Square of "hippies," or at least those "hippies" thought to be homosexuals, narcotics-users, or otherwise especially undesirable.

There have been throughout our history many analogous attempts to apply the police-power of government to protect the con-

ventional majority from too close association with the unpleasant
or undesirable minority. . . .

The Court held the police conduct unlawful but, in the belief
that city officials would prevent a recurrence of the violations,
declined to issue an injunction. The Court did, however, retain
jurisdiction and ordered that all records of the mass arrests be
expunged, and all photographs returned or destroyed.

Police misconduct will be reduced when cities and states pay
law enforcers higher salaries and demand, in return, better
qualified individuals. Nevertheless, the best qualified policeman
will not be a significant improvement unless the people who run
the departments and those to whom they listen bring the role of
the law enforcer closer to crime solving and crime prevention
and away from behavior control. So long as the police are used
to do illegally what society may not do legally, the Bill of Rights
is so much window-dressing and citizen distrust is inevitable.
However, as more qualified men fill positions whose duties are
better defined, we will begin to move away from the dangerous
situation Jerome Skolnick summarized in the *The Politics of
Protest:*

> The policeman in America is overworked, undertrained, under-
> paid, and undereducated. His job, moreover, is increasingly diffi-
> cult, forcing him into the almost impossible position of repressing
> deeply-felt demands for social and political change. In this role, he
> is unappreciated and at times despised.
> His difficulties are compounded by a view of protest that gives
> little consideration to the effects of such social factors as poverty
> and discrimination and virtually ignores the possibility of legiti-
> mate social discontent. Typically, it attributes mass protest instead
> to a conspiracy promulgated by agitators, often Communists, who
> mislead otherwise contented people. This view leaves the police ill-
> equipped to understand or deal with dissident groups.
> Given their social role and their ideology, the police have be-
> come increasingly frustrated, alienated, and angry. These emotions
> are being expressed in a growing militancy and political activism.
> The police are protesting. Police slowdowns and other forms of

strike activity, usually of questionable legality, have been to gain greater material benefits or changes in governmental policy (such as the "unleashing of the police"). Direct police challenges to departmental and civic authority have followed recent urban disorders, and criticisms of the judiciary have escalated to "court-watching" by police.

These developments are a part of a larger phenomenon—the emergence of the police as a self-conscious, independent political power. In many cities and states the police lobby rivals even duly elected officials in influence. Yet courts and police are expected to be neutral and nonpolitical, for even the perception of a lack of impartiality impairs public confidence in and reliance upon the legal system.

Police response to mass protest has often resulted in an escalation of conflict, hostility, and violence. The police violence during the Democratic National Convention in Chicago was not a unique phenomenon. We have found numerous other instances where violence has been initiated or exacerbated by police actions and attitudes, although violence also has been avoided by judicious planning and supervision.

Police violence is the antithesis of both law and order. It leads only to increased hostility, polarization, and violence—both in the immediate situation and in the future. Certainly it is clear today that effective policing ultimately depends upon the cooperation and goodwill of the policed, and these resources are quickly being exhausted by present attitudes and practices.

APPENDIX A

SUPREME COURT JUSTICES

(with year of appointment)

BURGER, WARREN	(1969)
BLACK, HUGO	(1937)
DOUGLAS, WILLIAM	(1939)
HARLAN, JOHN	(1954)
BRENNAN, WILLIAM	(1956)
STEWART, POTTER	(1958)
WHITE, BYRON	(1962)
MARSHALL, THURGOOD	(1967)
BLACKMUN, HARRY	(1970)

APPENDIX B

Selected Constitutional Amendments

Amendment IV [1791]

The right of the people to be secure in their persons, houses, papers, and effects, against unreasonable searches and seizures, shall not be violated, and no Warrants shall issue, but upon probable cause, supported by Oath or affirmation, and particularly describing the place to be searched, and the persons or things to be seized.

Amendment V [1791]

No person shall be held to answer for a capital, or otherwise infamous crime, unless on a presentment or indictment of a Grand Jury, except in cases arising in the land or naval forces, or in the Militia, when in actual service in time of War or public danger; nor shall any person be subject for the same offence to be twice put in jeopardy of life or limb; nor shall be compelled in any criminal case to be a witness against himself, nor be deprived of life, liberty, or property, without due process of law; nor shall private property be taken for public use, without just compensation.

Amendment VI [1791]

In all criminal prosecutions, the accused shall enjoy the right to a speedy and public trial, by an impartial jury of the State and district wherein the crime shall have been committed, which district shall have been previously ascertained by law, and to be informed of the nature and cause of the accusation; to be confronted with the witnesses against him; to have compulsory process for obtaining witnesses in his favor, and to have the Assistance of Counsel for his defence.

Amendment VIII [1791]

Excessive bail shall not be required, nor excessive fines imposed, nor cruel and unusual punishments inflicted.

Amendment XIV [1868]

Section 1. All persons born or naturalized in the United States, and subject to the jurisdiction thereof, are citizens of the United States and of the State wherein they reside. No State shall make or enforce any law which shall abridge the privileges or immunities of citizens of the United States; nor shall any State deprive any person of life, liberty, or property, without due process of law; nor deny to any person within its jurisdiction the equal protection of the laws.

Section 5. The Congress shall have power to enforce, by appropriate legislation, the provisions of this article.

A general view of The Criminal Justice System

This chart seeks to present a simple yet comprehensive view of the movement of cases through the criminal justice system. Procedures in individual jurisdictions may vary from the pattern shown here. The differing weights of line indicate the relative volumes of cases disposed of at various points in the system, but this is only suggestive since no nationwide data of this sort exists.

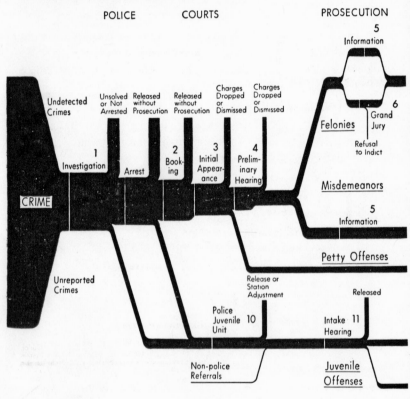

POLICE COURTS PROSECUTION

1 Investigation

2 Booking

3 Initial Appearance

4 Preliminary Hearing

5 Information

6 Grand Jury

10 Police Juvenile Unit

11 Intake Hearing

1 May continue until trial.

2 Administrative record of arrest. First step at which temporary release on bail may be available.

3 Before magistrate, commissioner, or justice of peace. Formal notice of charge, advice of rights. Bail set. Summary trials for petty offenses usually conducted here without further processing.

Preliminary testing of evidence against defendant. Charge may be reduced. No separate preliminary hearing for misdemeanors in some systems.

5 Charge filed by prosecutor on basis of information submitted by police or citizens. Alternative to grand jury indictment; often used in felonies, almost always in misdemeanors.

6 Reviews whether Government evidence sufficient to justify trial. Some States have no grand jury system; others seldom use it.

CORRECTIONS

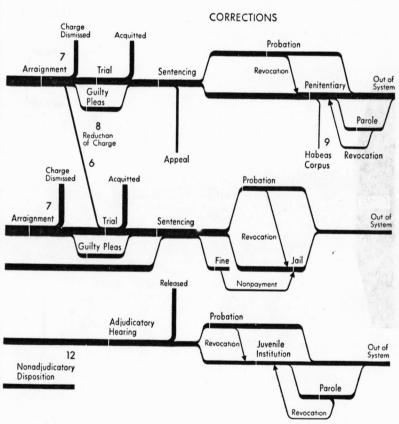

7 Appearance for plea; defendant elects trial by judge or jury (if available); counsel for indigent usually appointed here in felonies. Often not at all in other cases.

8 Charge may be reduced at any time prior to trial in return for plea of guilty or for other reasons.

9 Challenge on constitutional grounds to legality of detention. May be sought at any point in process.

10 Police often hold informal hearings, dismiss or adjust many cases without further processing.

11 Probation officer decides desirability of further court action.

12 Welfare agency, social services, counselling, medical care, etc., for cases where adjudicatory handling not needed.

INDEX